DATA CLEANING

DATA CLEANING
Pocket Primer

Oswald Campesato

MERCURY LEARNING AND INFORMATION
Dulles, Virginia
Boston, Massachusetts
New Delhi

Publisher: David Pallai
MERCURY LEARNING AND INFORMATION
22841 Quicksilver Drive
Dulles, VA 20166
info@merclearning.com
www.merclearning.com
800-232-0223

O. Campesato. *Data Cleaning Pocket Primer.*
ISBN: 978-1-68392-217-9

Library of Congress Control Number: 2017964301

181920321   Printed on acid-free paper in the United States of America

*I'd like to dedicate this book to my parents –
may this bring joy and happiness into their lives.*

CONTENTS

PREFACE: DATA CLEANING POCKET PRIMER

What Is the Goal?

The goal of this book is to introduce the reader to a powerful, flexible and free set of data manipulation and cleansing commands developed over decades in the unix/linux environment but are now available in any operating system with a minimum amount of effort to set up the environment. While all examples and scripts use the "bash" command set, many of the concepts translate into other forms of shell scripting (ksh, sh, csh), including the concept of piping data between commands, regular expression substitution and the sed and awk commands. Aimed at a reader relatively new to working in a bash environment, the book is comprehensive enough to be a good reference and teach a few new tricks to those who already have some experience with using shells scripts for data cleansing.

This short book contains a variety of code fragments and shell scripts for data scientists, data analysts, and other people who want shell-based solutions to "clean" various types of datasets.

This book takes introductory concepts and commands in bash, and then demonstrates their use in simple yet powerful shell scripts. This book does not cover "pure" system administration functionality for Unix or Linux. In general, topics that are not relevant in a shell-based Data Cleaning Pocket Primer are not covered in this book.

Is This Book for Me and What Will I Learn?

This book is intended for data scientists, data analysts, and other people who perform data cleaning tasks, and who also have a modest knowledge of shell programming.

You will acquire an understanding of how to use various bash commands, often as part of short shell scripts. The chapters also contain simple use cases that illustrate how to perform various tasks involving datasets, such as switching the order of a two-column dataset (Chapter 1), removing control characters in a text file (Chapter 2), find specific lines and merge them (Chapter 3), reformatting a date field in a dataset (Chapter 4), removing nested quotes (Chapter 5), along with supplemental code samples in the Appendix.

This book saves you the time required to search for relevant code samples, adapting them to your specific needs, which is a potentially time-consuming process.

How Were the Code Samples Created?

The code samples in this book were created and tested using bash on a Macbook Pro with OS X 10.12.6 (macOS Sierra). Regarding their content: the code samples are derived primarily from scripts prepared by the author, and in some cases there are code samples that incorporate short sections of code from discussions in online forums. The key point to remember is that the code samples follow the "Four Cs": they must be Clear, Concise, Complete, and Correct to the extent that it's possible to do so, given the size of this book.

What You Need to Know for This Book

You need some familiarity with working from the command line in a Unix-like environment. However, there are subjective prerequisites, such as a desire to learn shell programming, along with the motivation and discipline to read and understand the code samples. In any case, if you're not sure whether or not you can absorb the material in this book, glance through the code samples to get a feel for the level of complexity.

Which bash Commands are Excluded?

The commands that do not meet any of the criteria listed in the previous section are not included in this Primer. Consequently, there is no coverage of commands for system administration (e.g., shutting down a machine, scheduling backups, and so forth). The purpose of the material in the chapters is to illustrate how to use bash commands for handling common data cleaning tasks with datasets, after which you can do further reading to deepen your knowledge.

How Do I Set Up a Command Shell?

If you are a Mac user, there are three ways to do so. The first method is to use Finder to navigate to Applications > Utilities and then double click on the Utilities application. Next, if you already have a command shell available, you can launch a new command shell by typing the following command:

```
open /Applications/Utilities/Terminal.app
```

A second method for Mac users is to open a new command shell on a Macbook from a command shell that is already visible simply by clicking command+n in that command shell, and your Mac will launch another command shell.

If you are a PC user, you can install Cygwin (open source https://cygwin.com/) that simulates bash commands, or use another toolkit such as MKS (a commercial product). Please read the online documentation that describes the download and installation process.

If you use RStudio, you launch a command shell inside of RStudio by navigating to Tools > Command Line, and then you can launch bash commands. Note that custom aliases are not automatically set if they are defined in a file other than the main start-up file (such as .bash_login).

What Are the "Next Steps" after Finishing This Book?

The answer to this question varies widely, mainly because the answer depends heavily on your objectives. The best answer is to try a new tool or technique from the book out on a problem or task you care about, professionally or personally. Precisely what that might be depends on who you are, as the needs of a data scientist, manager, student, or developer are all different. In addition, keep what you learned in mind as you tackle new data cleaning or manipulation challenges. Sometimes knowing a technique is possible makes finding a solution easier, even if you have to re-read the section to remember exactly how the syntax works.

If you have reached the limits of what you have learned here and want to get further technical depth on these commands, there is a wide variety of literature published and online resources describing the bash shell, Unix programming, and the grep, sed, and awk commands.

ABOUT THE
TECHNICAL REVIEWER

Bradley Shanrock-Solberg has 30 years of experience in analytics in domains as diverse as freeway traffic flow, contracts management, warranty & returns, logistics, supply chain, game mechanics, software quality assurance, asynchronous messaging systems, commissions & sales support, order-to-cash processes, and volunteer management. Brad's career began at a traffic information startup, then he spent a few years as a business analyst, followed by 20 years in various IT roles at Seagate Technology. Since 2015, Brad has worked as a consulting data scientist in the San Francisco Bay area, helping clients learn to get the most value out of the data they own by using the tools they already understand. Brad is a certified Six Sigma Blackbelt and has a BS in engineering and applied science from the California Institute of Technology.

## CHAPTER 1

INTRODUCTION

This chapter introduces you to the bash shell. You will learn how to use some basic commands, such as navigating around the file system, listing files, and displaying the contents of files. This chapter is dense and contains a very eclectic mix of topics to quickly prepare you for later chapters. If you already have some knowledge of shell programming, you can probably skim quickly through this introductory chapter and proceed to Chapter 2.

The first part of this chapter starts with a brief introduction to some Unix shells, and then discusses files, file permissions, and directories. You will also learn how to create files and directories and how to change their permissions.

The second part of this chapter introduces simple shell scripts, along with instructions for making them executable. As you will see, shell scripts contain bash commands (and can optionally contain user-defined functions), so it's a good idea to learn about bash commands before you can create shell scripts (which include bash scripts).

The third portion of this chapter discusses two useful bash commands: the cut command (for cutting or extracting columns and/or fields from a dataset) and the paste command (for "pasting" text or datasets together vertically).

In addition, the final part of this chapter uses the material from the previous section (i.e., the cut command and paste command) in a use case that illustrates how to switch the order of two columns in a dataset. As you will see later, there are other ways to perform this task, such as invoking the awk command (discussed in Chapter 5).

There are a few points to keep in mind before delving into the details of shell scripts. First, shell scripts can be executed from the command line after adding "execute" permissions to the text file containing the shell script. Second, you can use the `crontab` utility to schedule the execution of your shell scripts. The `crontab` utility allows you to specify the execution of a shell script on an hourly, daily, weekly, or monthly basis. Tasks that are commonly scheduled via `crontab` include performing backups, removing unwanted files, and so forth. If you are completely new to Unix, just keep in mind that there is a way to run scripts both from the command line and in a "scheduled" manner. Setting file permissions to run the script from the command line will be discussed later.

Third, the contents of any shell script can be as simple as a single command, or can comprise hundreds of lines of bash commands. In general, the more interesting shell scripts involve a combination of several bash commands. A learning tip: since there are usually several ways to produce the desired result, it's helpful to read other people's shell scripts to learn how to combine commands in useful ways.

What Is Unix?

Unix is an operating system created by Ken Thompson in the early 1970s, and today there are several variants available, such as HP/UX for HP machines and AIX for IBM machines. Linus Torvalds developed the Linux operating system during the 1990s, and many Linux commands are the same as their bash counterparts (but differences exist, often in the commands for system administrators). The Mac OS X operating system is based on AT&T Unix.

Unix has a rich and storied history, and if you are really interested in learning about its past, you can read online articles and also Wikipedia. This book foregoes those details and focuses on helping you quickly learn how to become productive with various commands.

Available Shell Types

The original Unix shell is the Bourne shell, which was written in the mid-1970s by Stephen R. Bourne. In addition, the Bourne shell was the first shell to appear on bash systems, and you will sometimes hear "the shell" as a reference to the Bourne shell. The Bourne shell is a POSIX standard shell, usually installed as `/bin/sh` on most versions of Unix, whose default prompt is the $ character. Consequently, Bourne shell scripts will execute on almost every version of Unix. In essence, the AT&T branches of Unix support the Bourne shell (sh), bash, Korn shell (ksh), tsh, and zsh.

However, there is also the BSD branch of Unix that uses the "C" shell (csh), whose default prompt is the % character. In general, shell scripts written for csh will not execute on AT&T branches of Unix, unless the csh shell is also installed on those machines (and vice versa).

The Bourne shell is the most "unadorned" in the sense that it lacks some commands that are available in the other shells, such as history, noclobber, and so forth. The various subcategories for the Bourne Shell are listed as follows:

> Bourne shell (sh)
> Korn shell (ksh)
> Bourne Again shell (bash)
> POSIX shell (sh)

The different C-type shells follow:

> C shell (csh)
> TENEX/TOPS C shell (tcsh)

While the commands and the shell scripts in this book are based on the bash shell, many of the commands also work in other shells (and if not, those other shells have a similar command to accomplish the same goal). Performing an Internet search for "how do I do <bash command> in <shell name>" will often get you an answer. Sometimes the command is essentially the same, but with slightly different syntax, and typing "man <command>" in a command shell can provide useful information.

What Is bash?

Bash is an acronym for "Bourne Again Shell," which has its roots in the Bourne shell created by Stephen R. Bourne. Shell scripts based on the Bourne shell will execute in bash, but the converse is not true. The bash shell provides additional features that are unavailable in the Bourne shell, such as support for arrays (discussed later in this chapter).

On Mac OS X, the /bin directory contains the following executable shells:

```
-r-xr-xr-x  1 root   wheel   1377872  Apr 28   2017  /bin/ksh
-r-xr-xr-x  1 root   wheel    630464  Apr 28   2017  /bin/sh
-rwxr-xr-x  1 root   wheel    375632  Apr 28   2017  /bin/csh
-rwxr-xr-x  1 root   wheel    592656  Apr 28   2017  /bin/zsh
-r-xr-xr-x  1 root   wheel    626272  Apr 28   2017  /bin/bash
```

In case you're interested, a nice comparison matrix of the support for various features among the preceding shells is here:

https://stackoverflow.com/questions/5725296/difference-between -sh-and-bash.

Something else that might surprise you: in some environments the Bourne shell sh *is* the Bash shell, which you can check by typing the following command:

```
sh --version
GNU bash, version 3.2.57(1)-release (x86_64-apple-darwin16)
Copyright (C) 2007 Free Software Foundation, Inc.
```

If you are new to the command line (be it Mac, Linux, or PCs), please read the Preface, which provides some useful guidelines for accessing command shells.

Getting Help for bash Commands

If you want to see the options for a specific bash command, specify the -? switch. For example, cat -? displays the available options for the cat command. You can invoke the man command to see a description of a bash command and its options:

```
man cat
```

Keep in mind that the man command produces terse explanations, and if those explanations are not clear enough, you can search for online code samples that provide more details.

Navigating Around Directories

In a command shell you will often perform basic operations, such as displaying (or changing) the current directory, listing the contents of a directory, displaying the contents of a file, and so forth. The following set of commands shows you how to perform these operations, and you can execute a subset of these comments in the sequence that is relevant to you. Options for some of the commands in this section (such as the ls command) are described in greater detail later in this chapter.

A frequently used Bash command is pwd ("print working directory"), which displays the current directory, as shown here:

```
pwd
```

The output of the preceding command might look something like this:

```
/Users/jsmith
```

Use the cd ("change directory") command to go to a specific directory. For example, type the command cd /Users/jsmith/Mail or cd Mail if you are already in the /Users/jsmith directory. You can navigate to your home directory with either of these commands:

```
$ cd $HOME
$ cd
```

One convenient way to return to the previous directory is the command cd -. Keep in mind that the cd command on Windows merely displays the current directory (which differs from the Unix cd command).

The history Command

The history command displays the history of commands that you executed in the current command shell, as shown here:

```
history
```

A sample output of the preceding command is here:

```
1202  cat longfile.txt > longfile2.txt
1203  vi longfile2.txt
1204  cat longfile2.txt |fold -40
1205  cat longfile2.txt |fold -30
1206  cat longfile2.txt |fold -50
1207  cat longfile2.txt |fold -45
1208  vi longfile2.txt
1209  history
1210  cd /Library/Developer/CommandLineTools/usr/include/c++/
1211  cd /tmp
1212  cd $HOME/Desktop
1213  history
```

Now you can return to the directory in line 1210 with the following command:

```
!1210
```

The command !cd will search backward through the history of commands to find the first command that matches the cd command: in this case, line 1212 is the first match. If there weren't any intervening cd commands between the current command and the command in line 1210, then !1210 and !cd will have the same effect.

NOTE

Be careful with the "!" option with bash commands, because the command that matches the "!" might not be the one you intended, so it's safer to use the history command and then explicitly specify the correct number (in that history) when you invoke the "!" operator.

Listing Filenames with the `ls` Command

The `ls` command is for listing filenames, and there are many switches available that you can use, as shown in this section. For example, the `ls` command displays the following filenames (the actual display depends on the font size and the width of the command shell) on my Mac:

```
apple-care.txt         iphonemeetup.txt    outfile.txt        ssl-
instructions.txt    checkin-commands.txt    kyrgyzstan.txt
output.txt
```

The command `ls -1` (the digit "1") displays a vertical listing of filenames:

```
apple-care.txt
checkin-commands.txt
iphonemeetup.txt
kyrgyzstan.txt
outfile.txt
output.txt
ssl-instructions.txt
```

The command `ls -l` (the letter "l") displays a long listing of filenames:

```
total 56
-rwx------ 1 ocampesato staff  25 Jan 06 19:21 apple-care.txt
-rwx------ 1 ocampesato staff 146 Jan 06 19:21 checkin-commands.txt
-rwx------ 1 ocampesato staff 478 Jan 06 19:21 iphonemeetup.txt
-rwx------ 1 ocampesato staff  12 Jan 06 19:21 kyrgyzstan.txt
-rw-r--r-- 1 ocampesato staff  11 Jan 06 19:21 outfile.txt
-rw-r--r-- 1 ocampesato staff  12 Jan 06 19:21 output.txt
-rwx------ 1 ocampesato staff 176 Jan 06 19:21 ssl-instructions.txt
```

The command `ls -lt` (the letters "l" and "t") display a time-based long listing:

```
total 56
-rwx------1 ocampesato staff  25 Jan 06 19:21 apple-care.txt
-rwx------1 ocampesato staff 146 Jan 06 19:21 checkin-commands.txt
-rwx------1 ocampesato staff 478 Jan 06 19:21 iphonemeetup.txt
-rwx------1 ocampesato staff  12 Jan 06 19:21 kyrgyzstan.txt
-rw-r--r--1 ocampesato staff  11 Jan 06 19:21 outfile.txt
-rw-r--r--1 ocampesato staff  12 Jan 06 19:21 output.txt
-rwx------1 ocampesato staff 176 Jan 06 19:21 ssl-instructions.txt
```

The command `ls -ltr` (the letters "l", "t", and "r") display a reversed time-based long listing of filenames:

```
total 56
-rwx------1 ocampesato staff 176 Jan 06 19:21 ssl-instructions.txt
-rw-r--r--1 ocampesato staff  12 Jan 06 19:21 output.txt
```

```
-rw-r--r--1 ocampesato staff  11 Jan 06 19:21 outfile.txt
-rwx------1 ocampesato staff  12 Jan 06 19:21 kyrgyzstan.txt
-rwx------1 ocampesato staff 478 Jan 06 19:21 iphonemeetup.txt
-rwx------1 ocampesato staff 146 Jan 06 19:21 checkin-commands.txt
-rwx------1 ocampesato staff  25 Jan 06 19:21 apple-care.txt
```

Here is the description about all the listed columns in the preceding output:

Column #1: represents file type and permission given on the file (see the following)
Column #2: shows the number of memory blocks taken by the file or directory
Column #3: indicates the (Bash user) owner of the file
Column #4: represents group of the owner
Column #5: represents file size in bytes
Column #6: shows the date and time when this file was created or last modified
Column #7: represents file or directory name

In the ls -l listing example, every file line began with a d, -, or l. These characters indicate the type of file that's listed. These (and other) initial values are described as follows:

  -    Regular file (ASCII text file, binary executable, or hard link)
  b   Block special file (such as a physical hard drive)
  c   Character special file (such as a physical hard drive)
  d   Directory file that contains a listing of other files and directories
  l   Symbolic link file
  p   Named pipe (a mechanism for interprocess communications)
  s   Socket (for interprocess communication)

Consult online documentation for more details regarding the ls command.

Displaying Contents of Files

Now let's see how to display different lines of text in a text file. You can use the cat command to display the entire contents of a file, but it's a good idea to first get some information about the file contents. Specifically, use the wc (word count) command that displays the number of lines, words, and characters in a text file, as shown here:

```
wc longfile.txt
37      80      408 longfile.txt
```

The preceding output shows that the file `longfile.txt` contains 37 lines, 80 words, and 408 characters, which means that the file size is actually quite small (despite its name).

The `cat` Command

You can use the `cat` command to display the contents of `longfile.txt`:

```
cat longfile.txt
```

The preceding command displays the following text:

```
the contents
of this
long file
are too long
to see in a
single screen
and each line
contains
one or
more words
and if you
use the cat
command the
(other lines are omitted)
```

As another example, suppose that the file `temp1` has the following contents:

```
this is line1 of temp1
this is line2 of temp1
this is line3 of temp1
```

Suppose that the file `temp2` has these contents:

```
this is line1 of temp2
this is line2 of temp2
```

Now type the following command that contains the ? metacharacter (discussed in detail later in this chapter):

```
cat temp?
```

The output from the preceding command is shown here:

```
this is line1 of temp1
this is line2 of temp1
this is line3 of temp1
this is line1 of temp2
this is line2 of temp2
```

The head and tail Commands

The head command displays the first ten lines of a text file (by default), an example of which is here:

```
head longfile.txt
```

The preceding command displays the following text:

```
the contents
of this
long file
are too long
to see in a
single screen
and each line
contains
one or
more words
```

The head command also provides an option to specify a different number of lines to display, as shown here:

```
head -4 longfile.txt
```

The preceding command displays the following text:

```
the contents
of this
long file
are too long
```

The tail command displays the last ten lines (by default) of a text file:

```
tail longfile.txt
```

The preceding command displays the following text:

```
is available
in every shell
including the
bash shell
csh
zsh
ksh
and Bourne shell
```

NOTE *The last two lines in the preceding output are blank lines (not a typographical error in this page).*

Similarly, the `tail` command allows you to specify a different number of lines to display: `tail -4 longfile.txt` displays the last 4 lines of `longfile.txt`.

Use the `more` command to display a screenful of data, as shown here:

```
more longfile.txt
```

Press the `<spacebar>` to view the next screenful of data, and press the `<return>` key to see the next line of text in a file. Incidentally, some people prefer the `less` command, which generates essentially the same output as the `more` command. (A geeky joke: "What's less? It's more.")

The Pipe Symbol

A very useful feature of Bash is its support for the pipe symbol ("|") that enables you to "pipe" or redirect the output of one command to become the input of another command. The pipe command is very handy when you want to perform a sequence of operations involving various Bash commands.

For example, the following code snippet combines the `head` command with the `cat` command and the pipe ("|") symbol:

```
cat longfile.txt| head -2
```

A technical point: the preceding command creates two `bash` processes (more about processes later), whereas the command `head -2 longfile.txt` only creates a single `bash` process.

You can use the `head` and `tail` commands in more interesting ways. For example, the following command sequence displays lines 11 through 15 of `longfile.txt`:

```
head -15 longfile.txt |tail -5
```

The preceding command displays the following text:

```
and if you
use the cat
command the
file contents
scroll
```

Display the line numbers for the preceding output as follows:

```
cat -n longfile.txt | head -15 | tail -5
```

The preceding command displays the following text:

```
11    and if you
12    use the cat
13    command the
14    file contents
15    scroll
```

You won't see the "tab" character from the output, but it's visible if you redirect the previous command sequence to a file and then use the "-t" option with the cat command:

```
cat -n longfile.txt | head -15 | tail -5 > 1
cat -t 1
11^Iand if you
12^Iuse the cat
13^Icommand the
14^Ifile contents
15^Iscroll
```

The fold Command

The fold command enables you to "fold" the lines in a text file, which is useful for text files that contain long lines of text that you want to split into shorter lines. For example, here are the contents of longfile2.txt:

```
the contents of this long file are too long to see in a single
screen and each line contains one or more words and if you
use the cat command the file contents scroll off the screen so
you can use other commands such as the head or tail or more
commands in conjunction with the pipe command that is very
useful in Bash and is available in every shell including the
bash shell csh zsh ksh and Bourne shell
```

You can "fold" the contents of longfile2.txt into lines whose length is 45 (just as an example) with this command:

```
cat longfile2.txt |fold -45
```

The output of the preceding command is here:

```
the contents of this long file are too long t
o see in a single screen and each line contai
ns one or more words and if you use the cat c
ommand the file contents scroll off the scree
n so you can use other commands such as the h
ead or tail or more commands in conjunction w
ith the pipe command that is very useful in U
nix and is available in every shell including
the bash shell csh zsh ksh and Bourne shell
```

Notice that some words in the preceding output are split based on the line width, and not "newspaper style."

In Chapter 4 you will learn how to display the lines in a text file that match a string or a pattern, and in Chapter 5 you will learn how to replace a string with another string in a text file.

File Ownership: Owner, Group, and World

Bash files have `rwx` privileges, where `r` = read privilege, `w` = write privilege, `x` = execute privilege can be executed from the command line, simply by typing the file name (or the full path to file name if the file is not in your current directory). Invoking an executable file from the command line will cause the operating system to attempt to execute commands inside the text file.

Use the `chmod` command to set permissions for files. For example, if you need to set the permission `rwx  rw-  r--` for a file, use the following:

```
chmod u=rwx g=rw o=r filename
```

In the preceding command the options `u`, `g`, and `o` represent user permissions, group permissions, and other permissions, respectively.

In order to add additional permissions on the current file, use + to add permission to user, group, or others and use – to remove the permissions. For example, given a file with the permissions `rwx  rw-  r--`, add the executable permission as follows:

```
chmod o+x filename
```

This command adds the `x` permission for `others`.

Add the executable permission to all permission categories—that is, for user, group, and others—as follows:

```
chmod a+x filename
```

In the preceding command, the letter a means "all."

Specify a – in order to remove any permission, as shown here:

```
chmod a-x filename
```

Hidden Files

A so-called "invisible" file is one whose first character is the dot or period character (.). Bash programs (including the shell) use most of these files to store configuration information. Some common examples of hidden files include the following files:

.profile: the Bourne shell (sh) initialization script
.bash_profile: the bash shell (bash) initialization script
.kshrc: the Korn shell (ksh) initialization script
.cshrc: the C shell (csh) initialization script
.rhosts: the remote shell configuration file

To list invisible files, specify the -a option to ls:

```
ls -a
.              .profile      docs      lib      test_results
..             .rhosts       hosts     pub      users
.emacs         bin           hw1       res.01   work
.exrc          ch07          hw2       res.02
.kshrc         ch07.bak      hw3       res.03
```

Single dot .: This represents current directory.

Double dot ..: This represents parent directory.

Handling Problematic Filenames

Problematic filenames contain one or more whitespaces, hidden (non-printing) characters, or start with a dash ("-") character.

You can use double quotes to list filenames that contain whitespaces, or you can precede each whitespace by a backslash ("\") character.

For example, if you have a file named One Space.txt, you can use the ls command as follows:

```
ls -l "One Space.txt"
ls -l One\ Space.txt
```

Filenames that start with a dash ("-") character are difficult to handle because the dash character is the prefix that specifies options for bash commands. Consequently, if you have a file whose name is -abc, then the command ls -abc will not work correctly, because the "-a" is interpreted as a switch for the ls command (and there is no "a" option).

In most cases the best solution to this type of file is to rename the file. This can be done in your operating system if your client isn't a Unix shell, or you can use the following special syntax for the mv ("move") command to rename the file. The preceding two dashes tell mv to ignore the dash in the filename. An example is here:

```
mv -- -abc.txt renamed-abc.txt
```

Working with Environment Variables

There are many built-in environment variables available, and the following subsections discuss some of the more common variables.

The env Command

The env ("environment") command displays the variables that are in your bash environment. An example of the output of the env command is here:

```
SHELL=/bin/bash
TERM=xterm-256color
TMPDIR=/var/folders/73/39lngcln4dj_scmgvsv53g_w0000gn/T/
OLDPWD=/tmp
TERM_SESSION_ID=63101060-9DF0-405E-84E1-EC56282F4803
USER=ocampesato
COMMAND_MODE=bash2003PATH=/opt/local/bin:/Users/ocampesato/
android-sdk-mac_86/platform-tools:/Users/ocampesato/
android-sdk-mac_86/tools:/usr/local/bin:
PWD=/Users/ocampesato
JAVA_HOME=/System/Library/Java/JavaVirtualMachines/1.6.0.jdk/
Contents/Home
LANG=en_US.UTF-8
NODE_PATH=/usr/local/lib/node_modules
HOME=/Users/ocampesato
LOGNAME=ocampesato
DISPLAY=/tmp/launch-xnTgkE/org.macosforge.xquartz:0
SECURITYSESSIONID=186a4
_=/usr/bin/env
```

Some interesting examples of setting an environment variable and also executing a command are described here:

https://stackoverflow.com/questions/13998075/setting-environment-variable-for-one-program-call-in-bash-using-env.

Useful Environment Variables

This section discusses some important environment variables, most of which you probably will not need to modify, but it's useful to be aware of the existence of these variables and their purpose.

The HOME variable contains the absolute path of the user's home directory.

The HOSTNAME variable specifies the Internet name of the host.

The LOGNAME variable specifies the user's login name.

The PATH variable specifies the search path (see next subsection).

The SHELL variable specifies the absolute path of the current shell.

The USER specifies the user's current username. This value might be different than the login name if a superuser executes the su command to emulate another user's permissions.

Setting the PATH Environment Variable

Programs and other executable files can live in many directories, so operating systems provide a search path that lists the directories that the OS searches for executable files. Adding a directory to your path means an executable file can be called by just using the filename as a command, without having to call out its entire path, just as if it resided in your working directory.

The path is stored in an environment variable, which is a named string maintained by the operating system. These variables contain information available to the command shell and other programs.

The path variable is named PATH in bash or Path in Windows (bash is case-sensitive; Windows is not).

Setting the path in bash/Linux:

```
export PATH=$HOME/anaconda:$PATH
```

To add the Python directory to the path for a particular session in bash:

```
export PATH="$PATH:/usr/local/bin/python"
```

In Bourne shell or ksh shell enter this command:

```
PATH="$PATH:/usr/local/bin/python"
```

NOTE   /usr/local/bin *is the location of the* Python *executable*

Specifying Aliases and Environment Variables

The following command defines an environment variable called h1:

```
h1=$HOME/test
```

Now if you enter the following command:

```
echo $h1
```

you will see the following output on OS X:

```
/Users/jsmith/test
```

The next code snippet shows you how to set the alias `ll` so that it displays a long listing of a directory:

```
alias ll="ls -l"
```

The following three alias definitions involve the `ls` command and various switches:

```
alias ll="ls -l"
alias lt="ls -lt"
alias ltr="ls -ltr"
```

As an example, you can replace the command `ls -ltr` (the letters "l," "t," and "r") that you saw earlier in the chapter with the `ltr` alias, and you will see the same reversed time-based long listing of filenames (reproduced here):

```
total 56
-rwx------ 1 ocampesato staff 176 Jan 06 19:21 ssl-instructions.txt
-rw-r--r-- 1 ocampesato staff  12 Jan 06 19:21 output.txt
-rw-r--r-- 1 ocampesato staff  11 Jan 06 19:21 outfile.txt
-rwx------ 1 ocampesato staff  12 Jan 06 19:21 kyrgyzstan.txt
-rwx------ 1 ocampesato staff 478 Jan 06 19:21 iphonemeetup.txt
-rwx------ 1 ocampesato staff 146 Jan 06 19:21 checkin-commands.txt
-rwx------ 1 ocampesato staff  25 Jan 06 19:21 apple-care.txt
```

You can also define an alias that contains the Bash pipe ("|") symbol:

```
alias ltrm="ls -ltr|more"
```

In a similar manner, you can define aliases for directory related commands:

```
alias ltd="ls -lt | grep '^d'"
alias ltdm="ls -lt | grep '^d'|more"
```

Finding Executable Files

There are several commands available for finding executable files (binary files or shell scripts) by searching the directories in the PATH environment variable: which, whence, whereis, and whatis. These commands produce results similar to the which command, as discussed below.

The which command gives the full path to whatever executable that you specify or a blank line if the executable is not in any directory that is specified in the PATH environment variable. This is useful for finding out whether a particular command or utility is installed on the system.

```
which rm
```

The output of the preceding command is here:

```
/usr/bin/rm
```

The whereis command provides the information that you get from the where command, and also the location of the man page of the executable:

```
$ whereis rm
rm: /bin/rm /usr/share/man/man1/rm.1.bz2
```

The whatis command looks up the specified command in the whatis database, which is useful for identifying system commands and important configuration files. Consider it a simplified "man" command, which displays concise details about bash commands (e.g., type man ls and you will see several pages of explanation regarding the ls command).

What Are Shell Scripts?

Shell scripts contain bash commands, which are executed sequentially from top to bottom (i.e., in the sequence that they appear in a shell script), unless they are defined inside a function. In particular, user-defined functions in shell scripts are executed in the order that they are *invoked* instead of in the order that they *appear* in the shell script. However, you can change the sequence in which commands are executed by using conditional logic, case statements, loops, and functions.

Shell scripts can contain whatever bash commands are available on your system (but be aware that some commands require the sudo command, which in turn requires a password). Simple examples of shell scripts include file-related commands that create files, read data from files, and update the contents of files. Regardless of the contents of your shell scripts, they are interpreted "on the fly," so there are no compilation steps that create a binary executable.

The purpose of shell scripts is to automate the process of executing a set of bash commands so that you don't need to execute them manually from the command line. If you need to execute a simple command from the command line, then it's unlikely that you need to do so via a shell script: just type the command and press the <RETURN> key. Note that the `bash crontab` utility enables you to schedule the execution of shell scripts at various points in time (the `crontab` utility is outside the scope of this book).

As you probably know, comments are important in source code. A good shell script contains meaningful comments, which are preceded by a pound sign "#," that explain the purpose of different sections in the shell script. The exception is when the "#" symbol appears in the first line of a shell script, as you will see in the next section.

A Simple Shell Script

Create the file `test.sh` (using your favorite text editor) with the following contents:

```
#!/bin/bash
pwd
ls
cd /tmp
ls
mkdir /tmp/abc
touch /tmp/abc/emptyfile
ls /tmp/abc/
```

Now save the above content and make this script executable as follows:

```
chmod +x test.sh
```

Now you have your shell script ready to be executed as follows:

```
./test.sh
```

NOTE *The output from launching `test.sh` depends on the contents of the `/tmp` directory.*

The first line in `test.sh` is called the "shebang" line, which directs the system to launch the bash shell in order to invoke the commands in `test.sh`. The term shebang is sort of a contraction of "hash" (for the "#" character) and "bang" (for the "!" character). Note that the initial "./" of `./test.sh` specifies the file `test.sh` in the current directory: if the file `test.sh` is in your home directory, specify `$HOME/test.sh`. In addition, if "." is included in the `PATH` environment variable, then you can simply type `test.sh` without the "./" prefix.

One point regarding the `mkdir` command: if you specify a path in which intermediate directories do not exist, then you need to use the `-p` switch. For example, if the directory /tmp/abc does not exist, then the following command requires the `-p` switch:

```
mkdir -p /tmp/abc/def
```

As another example of a simple shell script, the following script uses the `read` command, which takes the input from the keyboard and assigns that input value as the value of the variable PERSON. The `echo` command prints the input value on STDOUT, which is the screen (by default).

```
#!/bin/sh
echo "What is your name?"
read PERSON
echo "Hello, $PERSON"
```

Here is sample invocation of this script:

```
$./test.sh
What is your name?
John Smith
Hello, John Smith
```

Using a Semicolon to Separate Commands

You can combine multiple commands with a semicolon (";"), as shown here:

```
cd /tmp; pwd; cd ~; pwd
```

The preceding code snippet navigates to the /tmp directory, prints the full path to the current directory, returns to the previous directory, and again prints the full path to the current directory. The output of the preceding command is here:

```
/tmp
/Users/jsmith
```

You can use command substitution (discussed in a later section) to assign the output to a variable, as shown here:

```
x=`cd /tmp; pwd; cd ~; pwd`
echo $x
```

The output of the preceding snippet is here:

```
/tmp /Users/jsmith
```

The `printf` Command and the `echo` Command

In brief, use the `printf` command instead of the `echo` command if you need to control the output format. One key difference is that the `echo` command prints a newline character whereas the `printf` statement does not print a newline character. Keep this point in mind when you see the `printf` statement in the `awk` code samples in Chapter 5.

As a simple example, place the following code snippet in a shell script:

```
printf "%-5s %-10s %-4s\n" ABC DEF GHI
printf "%-5s %-10s %-4.2f\n" ABC DEF 12.3456
```

Make the shell script executable and then launch the shell script, after which you will see the following output:

```
ABC   DEF        GHI
ABC   DEF        12.35
```

On the other hand, if you type the following pair of commands:

```
echo "ABC DEF GHI"
echo "ABC DEF 12.3456"
```

you will see the following output:

```
ABC DEF GHI
ABC DEF 12.3456
```

A detailed (and very lengthy) discussion regarding the `printf` statement and the `echo` command is here:

https://unix.stackexchange.com/questions/65803/why-is-printf-better-than-echo.

The `echo` Command and Whitespaces

The `echo` command preserves whitespaces in variables, but in some cases the results might be different from your expectations.

Listing 1.1 displays the contents of `EchoCut.sh` that illustrates the differences that can occur when the `echo` command is used with the `cut` command.

LISTING 1.1. EchoCut.sh

```
x1="123    456    789"
x2="123 456 789"
echo "x1 = $x1"
echo "x2 = $x2"


x3=`echo $x1    | cut -c1-7`
x4=`echo "$x1"  | cut -c1-7`
x5=`echo $x2    | cut -c1-7`
echo "x3 = $x3"
echo "x4 = $x4"
echo "x5 = $x5"
```

Launch the code in Listing 1.1 and you will see the following output:

```
x1 = 123    456    789
x2 = 123 456 789
x3 = 123 456
x4 = 123    4
x5 = 123 456
```

The value of x3 is probably different from what you expected: there is only one blank space between 123 and 456 instead of the three blank spaces that appear in the definition of the variable x1.

This seemingly minor detail is important when you write shell scripts that check the values contained in specific columns of text files, such as payroll files and other files with financial data. The solution involves the use of double quote marks (and sometimes the IFS variable that is discussed in Chapter 2) that you can see in the definition of x4.

Command Substitution ("back tick")

The "back tick" or command substitution feature of the Bourne shell is very powerful and enables you to combine multiple bash commands. You can also write very compact and powerful (and complicated) shell scripts with command substitution. The syntax is to simply precede and follow your command with a "`" (back tick) character. In Listing 1.2, the back tick command is `ls *py`

Listing 1.2 displays the contents of CommandSubst.sh that displays a subset of the list of files in a directory.

LISTING 1.2. CommandSubst.sh

```
for f in `ls *py`
do
   echo "file is: $f"
done
```

Listing 1.2 contains a `for` loop that displays the filenames (in the current directory) that have a "py" suffix.

The output of Listing 1.2 on my MacBook is here:

```
file is: CapitalizeList.py
file is: CompareStrings.py
file is: FixedColumnCount1.py
file is: FixedColumnWidth1.py
file is: LongestShortest1.py
file is: My2DMatrix.pyß
file is: PythonBash.py
file is: PythonBash2.py
file is: StringChars1.py
file is: Triangular1.py
file is: Triangular2.py
file is: Zip1.py
```

NOTE *The output depends on whether or not you have any files with a* `.py` *suffix in the directory where you execute* `CommandSubst.sh`*.*

Setting Environment Variables via Shell Scripts

A very important concept when using shell scripts is that any variables set inside the script are no longer set when the script finishes executing. The rules are shown as follows:

- If a variable isn't set in a script, but is already defined before the script is executed, that variable will also be available inside the script.
- If a variable is set in a script, it will override any existing variable with the same name after the variable is set, but once the script ends, the variable will revert to its old value (or to no value, if it did not exist outside the shell script).

For example, if your `$HOME` directory is `/Users/jsmith`, but inside a script on row 10 you define `$HOME` to be `/Users/common/bin`, then the value of `$HOME` is initially `/Users/jsmith` for rows 1–9, then becomes `/Users/common/bin` on row 10, and maintains that value until the last command in the shell script is executed. Then the value reverts to `/Users/jsmith`.

The reason for this behavior is related to how Unix structures its processes (known as "shells," hence the term "shell script"). That discussion is beyond the scope of this book.

Therefore, the default behavior is that if you set the value of a variable in a shell script, then that variable (and its value) exist only for the duration of the execution of the shell script. There is a simple "workaround" whereby variables "hold" their values after a shell script has completed, and you'll learn how to do so in a subsequent section.

Just to make sure that the distinction is clear, consider Listing 1.3 that displays the contents of the shell script abc.sh.

LISTING 1.3. abc.sh

```
export x="123"
echo "inside abc.sh"
echo "x = $x"
```

Make sure that abc.sh is an executable shell script with the chmod command (as shown earlier in this chapter) and then launch the following sequence of commands from the command line:

```
export x="tom"
echo "x = $x"
./abc.sh
echo "x = $x"
```

The output from the preceding commands is here:

```
x = tom
inside abc.sh
x = 123
x = tom
```

As you can see, the value that is assigned to the variable x is only for the duration of the process associated with the shell script abc.sh. After execution has competed, the process terminates and the value of x reverts to its original value. Fortunately, there is a way to ensure that the values of variables in a shell script can be "set" for the current shell, a technique called "sourcing" the shell script, as described in the next section.

Sourcing or "Dotting" a Shell Script

Now execute the following sequence of commands:

```
export x="tom smith"
echo "x = $x"
. abc.sh
echo "x = $x"
```

The output from the preceding commands is here:

```
x = "tom smith"
inside abc.sh
x = 123
x = 123
```

In the preceding code block, the value assigned to the variable x inside the shell script abc.sh overrides its previously defined value because "sourcing" (also called "dotting") a shell script does not create a new process. Consequently, if a shell script assigns a new value to an existing variable, that new value is placed in the current environment and the previously defined value is lost.

Working with Arrays

Arrays are critical to data management and appear in a variety of real world contexts. It is a common problem to want to group related data elements together, then reference it within a row.

For example, at a volunteer event you might have to sign in and provide your name, address, and phone number so they can contact you later for future events. That related data could be thought of (and defined in bash) as:

```
volunteer[0] = name
volunteer[1] = Address
volunteer[2] = phone number
```

The sign-in list could be then captured as a file that used an internal field separator [IFS] to make each row a volunteer, and each data element (name, address, phone number) distinct, easy to use with a later bash script (or any other programming language or program that understands the concept of IFS).

The IFS is a concept covered in detail in Chapter 2, but it will be used in the following examples so you get a taste of how it is used. If you are familiar with ".csv" (comma separated value) text output from spreadsheets, the comma in those files is the IFS. If you were to open the sign-in list in an Excel spreadsheet or Google Doc created with commas as IFS, you would have column A = name, column B = address, and column C = phone number, each row a separate volunteer.

This section contains several shell scripts that illustrate some useful features of arrays in bash. Listing 1.4 displays the contents of array1.sh, which illustrates how to use an array and some operations that you can perform on arrays.

The syntax in bash is different enough from other programming languages that it's worthwhile to use several examples to explore its behavior.

LISTING 1.4. array1.sh

```
#!/bin/bash

# method #1:
fruits[0]="apple"
fruits[1]="banana"
fruits[2]="cherry"
fruits[3]="orange"
fruits[4]="pear"
echo "first fruit: ${fruits[0]}"

# method #2:
declare -a fruits2=(apple banana cherry orange pear)
echo "first fruit: ${fruits2[0]}"

# range of elements:
echo "last two: ${fruits[@]:3:2}"

# substring of element:
echo "substring: ${fruits[1]:0:3}"

arrlength=${#fruits[@]}
echo "length: ${#fruits[@]}"
```

Listing 1.5 displays the contents of names.txt and Listing 1.6 displays the contents of array-from-file.sh, which contains a for loop to iterate through the elements of an array whose initial values are based on the contents of names.txt.

LISTING 1.5. names.txt

```
Jane Smith
John Jones
Dave Edwards
```

LISTING 1.6. array-from-file.sh

```
#!/bin/bash

names="names.txt"
contents1=( `cat "$names"` )

echo "First loop:"
for w in "${contents1[@]}"
do
  echo "$w"
done
```

```
IFS=""
names="names.txt"
contents1=( `cat "$names"` )

echo "Second loop:"
for w in "${contents1[@]}"
do
  echo "$w"
done
```

Listing 1.6 initializes the array variable `contents1` by using command substitution with the `cat` command, followed by a loop that displays elements of the array `contents1`. The second for loop is the same code as the first for loop, but this time with the value of `IFS` equal to "", which has the effect of using the newline as a separator, one data element per row.

Launch the code in Listing 1.6 and you will see the following output:

```
First loop:
Jane
Smith
John
Jones
Dave
Edwards
Second loop:
Jane Smith
John Jones
Dave Edwards
```

Listing 1.7 displays the contents of `array-function.sh`, which illustrates how to initialize an array and then display its contents in a user-defined function.

LISTING 1.7. array-function.sh

```
#!/bin/bash

# compact version of the code later in this script:
#items() { for line in "${@}" ; do printf "%s\n" "${line}" ;
done ; }
#aa=( 7 -4 -e ) ; items "${aa[@]}"

items() {
  for line in "${@}"
  do
    printf "%s\n" "${line}"
  done
}

arr=( 123 -abc 'my data' )
items "${arr[@]}"
```

Listing 1.7 contains the items() function that displays the contents of the arr array that has been initialized prior to invoking this function. The output is shown here:

```
123
-abc
my data
```

Listing 1.8 displays the contents of array-loops1.sh, which illustrates how to determine the length of an initialized array and then display its contents via a for loop.

LISTING 1.8. array-loops1.sh

```
#!/bin/bash

fruits[0]="apple"
fruits[1]="banana"
fruits[2]="cherry"
fruits[3]="orange"
fruits[4]="pear"

# array length:
arrlength=${#fruits[@]}
echo "length: ${#fruits[@]}"

# print each element via a loop:
for (( i=1; i<${arrlength}+1; i++ ));
do
   echo "element $i of ${arrlength} : " ${fruits[$i-1]}
done
```

Listing 1.8 contains straightforward code for initializing an array and displaying its values.

Working with Nested Loops

This section is mainly for fun: you will see how to use nested loops to display a "triangular" output. Listing 1.9 displays the contents of nested-loops.sh, which illustrates how to display an alternating set of symbols in a triangular fashion.

LISTING 1.9. nestedloops2.sh

```
#!/bin/bash

outermax=10
symbols[0]="#"
symbols[1]="@"
```

```
for (( i=1; i<${outermax}; i++ ));
do
   for (( j=1; j<${i}; j++ ));
   do
     printf "%-2s" ${symbols[($i+$j)%2]}
   done
   printf "\n"
done
for (( i=1; i<${outermax}; i++ ));
do
   for (( j=${i}+1; j<${outermax}; j++ ));
   do
     printf "%-2s" ${symbols[($i+$j)%2]}
   done
   printf "\n"
done
```

Listing 1.9 initializes some variables, followed by a nested loop. The outer loop is "controlled" by the loop variable i, whereas the inner loop (which depends on the value of i) is "controlled" by the loop variable j. The key point to notice is how the following code snippet prints alternating symbols in the symbols array, depending on whether or not the value of $i + $j is even or odd:

```
printf "%-2s" ${symbols[($i+$j)%2]}
```

You can easily generalize this code: if the symbols array contains arrlength elements, then replace the preceding code snippet with the following:

```
printf "%-2s" ${symbols[($i+$j)% $arrlength]}
```

Launch the code in Listing 1.9 and you will see the following output:

```
@
# @
@ # @
# @ # @
@ # @ # @
# @ # @ # @
@ # @ # @ # @
# @ # @ # @ # @
@ # @ # @ # @ #
@ # @ # @ # @
@ # @ # @ #
@ # @ # @
@ # @ #
@ # @
@ #
@
```

The `paste` Command

The `paste` command is useful when you need to combine two files in a "pairwise" fashion. For example, Listing 1.10 and Listing 1.11 display the contents of the text files `list1` and `list2`, respectively. You can think of `paste` as adding the contents of the second file as a new column in the first file. In our first example, the first file has a list of files to copy, and the second file has a list of files that are the destination for the copy command. Paste then merges the two files into output that could then be run to execute all the copy commands in one step.

LISTING 1.10. list1

```
cp abc.sh
cp abc2.sh
cp abc3.sh
```

LISTING 1.11. list2

```
def.sh
def2.sh
def3.sh
```

Listing 1.12 displays the result of invoking the following command:

```
paste list1 list2 >list1.sh
```

LISTING 1.12. list1.sh

```
cp abc.sh     def.sh
cp abc2.sh    def2.sh
cp abc3.sh    def3.sh
```

Listing 1.12 contains three `cp` commands that are the result of invoking the paste command. If you want to execute the commands in Listing 1.12, make this shell script executable and then launch the script, as shown here:

```
chmod +x list1.sh
./list1.sh
```

Inserting Blank Lines with the `paste` Command

Instead of merging two equal length files, `paste` can also be used to add the same thing to every line in a file. This example inserts a blank line after every line in `names.txt` with this command:

```
paste -d'\n' - /dev/null < names.txt
```

The output is here:

```
Jane Smith

John Jones

Dave Edwards
```

Insert a blank line after every other line in `names.txt` with this command:

```
paste -d'\n' - - /dev/null < names.txt
```

The output is here:

```
Jane Smith
John Jones

Dave Edwards
```

Insert a blank line after every third line in `names.txt` with this command:

```
paste -d'\n' - - - /dev/null < names.txt
```

The output is here:

```
Jane Smith
John Jones
Dave Edwards
```

Note that there is a blank line after the third line in the preceding output. The shell script `joinlines.sh` (later in this chapter) also contains examples of one-line paste commands for joining consecutive lines of a dataset or text file.

The cut Command

The `cut` command enables you to extract fields with a specified delimiter (another word commonly used for `IFS`, especially when it's part of a command syntax, instead of being set as an outside variable) as well as a range of columns from an input stream. Some examples are here:

```
x="abc def ghi"
echo $x | cut -d" " -f2
```

The output (using space " " as `IFS`, and `-f2` to indicate the second column) of the preceding code snippet is here:

```
def
```

Consider this code snippet:

```
x="abc def ghi"
echo $x | cut -c2-5
```

The output of the preceding code snippet (-c2-5 means extract the characters in columns 2 through 5 from the variable) is here:

```
bc d
```

Listing 1.13 displays the contents of SplitName1.sh, which illustrates how to split a filename containing the "." character as a delimiter/IFS.

LISTING 1.13. SplitName1.sh

```
fileName="06.22.04p.vp.0.tgz"

f1=`echo $fileName | cut -d"." -f1`
f2=`echo $fileName | cut -d"." -f2`
f3=`echo $fileName | cut -d"." -f3`
f4=`echo $fileName | cut -d"." -f4`
f5=`echo $fileName | cut -d"." -f5`

f5=`expr $f5 + 12`

newFileName="${f1}.${f2}.${f3}.${f4}.${f5}"
echo "newFileName: $newFileName"
```

Listing 1.13 uses the echo command and the cut command in order to initialize the variables f1, f2, f3, f4, and f5, after which a new filename is constructed. The output of the preceding shell script is here:

```
newFileName: 06.22.04p.vp.12
```

Working with Metacharacters

Metacharacters can be thought of as a complex set of wildcards. Regular expressions are a "search patterns" which are a combination of normal text and metacharacters. In concept it is much like a "find" tool (press ctrl-f on your search engine), but bash (and Unix in general) allows for much more complex pattern matching because of its rich metacharacter set. There are entire books devoted to regular expressions, but this section contains enough information to get started, and the key concepts needed for data manipulation and cleansing.

The following metacharacters are useful with regular expressions:

The ? metacharacter refers to 0 or 1 occurrences of something.

The + metacharacter refers to 1 or more occurrences of something.

The * metacharacter refers to 0 more occurrences of something.

Note that "something" in the preceding descriptions can refer to a digit, letter, word, or more complex combinations.

Some examples are shown here:

The expression a? matches zero or one occurrences of the letter a.

The expression a+ matches the string a followed by one or more occurrences of anything.

The expression a* matches the string a followed by zero or more occurrences of anything.

The pipe "|" metacharacter (which has a different context from the pipe symbol in the command line: regular expressions have their own syntax, which does not match that of the operating system a lot of the time) provides a choice of options. For example, the expression a|b means a or b, and the expression a|b|c means a or b or c.

The "$" metacharacter refers to the end of a line of text, and in regular expressions inside the vi editor, the "$" metacharacter refers to the last line in a file.

The "^" metacharacter refers to the beginning of a string or a line of text. For example:

```
^a$ matches "Mary Anna" but not "Anna Mary"
^A* matches "Anna Mary" but not "Mary Anna"
```

In the case of regular expressions, the "^" metacharacter can also mean "does not match." The next section contains some examples of the "^" metacharacter.

Working with Character Classes

Character classes enable you to express a range of digits, letters, or a combination of both. For example, the character class [0-9] matches any single digit; [a-z] matches any lowercase letter; and [A-Z] matches any uppercase letter. You can also specify subranges of digits or letters, such as [3-7], [g-p], and [F-X], as well as other combinations:

[0-9][0-9] matches a consecutive pair of digits

[0-9][0-9][0-9] matches three consecutive digits

\d{3} also matches three consecutive digits

The previous section introduced you to the "^" metacharacter, and here are some examples of using "^" with character classes:

1) ^[a-z] matches any lowercase letter at the beginning of a line of text
2) ^[^a-z] matches any line of text that does *not* start with a lowercase letter

Based on what you have learned thus far, you can understand the purpose of the following regular expressions:

3) ([a-z]|[A-Z]): either a lowercase letter or an uppercase letter
4) (^[a-z][a-z]): an initial lowercase letter followed by another lowercase letter
5) (^[^a-z][A-Z]): anything other than a lowercase letter followed by an uppercase letter

Chapter 4 contains a section that discusses regular expressions, which combine character classes and metacharacters in order to create sophisticated expressions for matching complex string patterns (such as email addresses).

The "pipe" Symbol and Multiple Commands

At this point you've seen various combinations of bash commands that are connected with the "|" symbol. The general form looks something like this:

```
cmd1 | cmd2 | cmd3 …. >mylist
```

What happens if there are intermediate errors? You've seen how to redirect error messages to /dev/null, and you can also redirect error messages to a text file if you need to review them. Yet another option is to redirect stderr ("standard error") to stdout ("standard out"), which is beyond the scope of this chapter.

Question: can an intermediate error cause the entire "pipeline" to fail? Unfortunately, this scenario can occur, and in general it's a trial-and-error process to debug long and complex commands that involve multiple pipe symbols.

Now consider the case where you need to redirect the output of multiple commands to the same location. For example, the following commands display output on the screen:

```
ls | sort; echo "the contents of /tmp: "; ls /tmp
```

You can easily redirect the output to a file with this command:

```
(ls | sort; echo "the contents of /tmp:"; ls /tmp) > myfile1
```

However, each of the preceding commands inside the parentheses spawns a subshell (which is an extra process that consumes memory and cpu). You can avoid spawning subshells by using { } instead of (), as shown here (and the whitespaces after { and before } are required):

```
{ ls | sort; echo "the contents of /tmp:"; ls /tmp } > myfile1
```

Suppose that you want to set a variable and execute a command, and then invoke a second command via a pipe, as shown here:

```
name=SMITH cmd1 | cmd2
```

Unfortunately, cmd2 in the preceding code snippet does not recognize the value of name, but there is a simple solution, as shown here:

```
(name=SMITH cmd1) | cmd2
```

Use the double ampersand && symbol if you want to execute a command only if a prior command succeeds. For example, the cd command only works if the mkdir command succeeds in the following code snippet:

```
mkdir /tmp2/abc && cd /tmp2/abc
```

The preceding command will fail because (by default) the /tmp2 does not exist. On the other hand, the following command succeeds because the -p option ensures that intermediate directories are created:

```
mkdir -p /tmp/abc/def && cd /tmp/abc && ls -l
```

A Simple Use Case

The code sample in this section shows you how to use the paste command in order to join consecutive rows in a dataset. Listing 1.14 displays the contents of linepairs.csv, which contains letter and number pairs, and Listing 1.15 contains reversecolumns.sh, which illustrates how to match the pairs even though the line breaks are in different places between numbers and letters.

LISTING 1.14. *linepairs.csv*

```
a,b,c,d,e,f,g
h,i,j,k,l
1,2,3,4,5,6,7,8,9
10,11,12
```

LISTING 1.15. *linepairs.sh*

```
inputfile="linepairs.csv"
outputfile="linepairsjoined.csv"

# join pairs of consecutive lines:
paste -d " "   - - < $inputfile > $outputfile

# join three consecutive lines:
#paste -d " "   - - - < $inputfile > $outputfile

# join four consecutive lines:
#paste -d " "   - - - - < $inputfile > $outputfile
```

The contents of the output file are shown here (note that the script is just joining pairs of lines; the three- and four-line command examples are commented out):

```
a,b,c,d,e,f,g h,i,j,k,l
1,2,3,4,5,6,7,8,9 10,11,12
```

Notice that the preceding output is not completely correct: there is a space " " instead of a "," whenever a pair of lines is joined (between "g" and "h" and "9" and "10"). We can make the necessary revision using the sed command (discussed in Chapter 4):

```
cat $outputfile | sed "s/ /,/g" > $outputfile2
```

Examine the contents of $outputfile2 to see the result of the preceding code snippet.

Another Simple Use Case

The code sample in this section shows you how to use the cut and paste commands in order to reverse the order of two columns in a dataset. Keep in mind that the purpose of the shell script in Listing 1.17 is to help you get some practice for writing bash scripts. The better solution involves a single line of code (shown at the end of this section).

Listing 1.16 displays the contents of namepairs.csv, which contains the first name and last name of a set of people, and Listing 1.17 contains reversecolumns.sh, which illustrates how to reverse these two columns.

LISTING 1.16. namepairs.csv

```
Jane,Smith
Dave,Jones
Sara,Edwards
```

LISTING 1.17. reversecolums.sh

```
inputfile="namepairs.csv"
outputfile="reversenames.csv"
fnames="fnames"
lnames="lnames"

cat $inputfile|cut -d"," -f1 > $fnames
cat $inputfile|cut -d"," -f2 > $lnames

paste -d"," $lnames $fnames > $outputfile
```

The contents of the output file are shown here:

```
Smith,Jane
Jones,Dave
Edwards,Sara
```

The code in Listing 1.17 (after removing blank lines) consists of seven lines of code that involves creating two extra intermediate files. Unless you need those files, it's a good idea to remove those two files (which you can do with one rm command).

Although Listing 1.17 is straightforward, there is a simpler way to execute this task: use the cat command and the awk command (discussed in detail in Chapter 5).

Specifically, compare the contents of reversecolumns.sh with the following single line of code that combines the cat command and the awk command in order to generate the same output:

```
cat namepairs.txt |awk -F"," '{print $2 "," $1}'
```

The output from the preceding code snippet is here:

```
Smith,Jane
Jones,Dave
Edwards,Sara
```

As you can see, there is a big difference in these two solutions. If you are unfamiliar with the `awk` command, then obviously you would not have thought of the second solution. However, the more you learn about `bash` commands and how to combine them, the more adept you will become in terms of writing better shell scripts to solve data cleaning tasks. Another important point: document the commands as they get more complex, as they can be hard to interpret later by others, or even by yourself if enough time has passed. A comment like the following can be extremely helpful to interpreting code:

```
# This command reverses first and last names in namepairs.txt
cat namepairs.txt |awk -F"," '{print $2 "," $1}'
```

Summary

This chapter started with an introduction to some Unix shells, followed by a brief discussion of files, file permissions, and directories. You also learned how to create files and directories and how to change their permissions. Next you learned about environment variables, how to set them, and also how to use aliases. You also learned about "sourcing" (also called "dotting") a shell script and how this changes variable behavior from calling a shell script in the normal fashion.

Next you learned about the `cut` command (for cutting columns and/or fields) and the `paste` command (for "pasting" test together vertically). Finally, you saw two use cases, the first of which involved the `cut` command and `paste` command to switch the order to two columns in a dataset, and the second showed you another way to perform the same task using concepts from later chapters.

CHAPTER 2

USEFUL COMMANDS

This chapter discusses various bash commands that you can use when working with datasets, such as splitting, sorting, and comparing datasets. You see examples of finding files in a directory and then searching for strings in those files using the bash "pipe" command that redirects the output of one bash command as the input of a second bash command.

The first part of this chapter shows you how to merge, fold, and split datasets. This section also shows you how to sort files and find unique lines in files using the sort and uniq commands, respectively. The last portion explains how to compare text files and binary files.

The second section introduces you to the find command, which is a powerful command that supports many options. For example, you can search for files in the current directory or in subdirectories; you can search for files based on their creation date and last modification date. One convenient combination is to "pipe" the output of the find command to the xargs command in order to search files for a particular pattern. Next you will see how to use the tr command, a tool which handles a lot of commonly used text transformations such as capitalization or removal of whitespace. After the section that discusses the tr command you will see a use case that shows you how use the tr command in order to remove the ^M control character from a dataset.

The third section contains compression-related commands, such as cpio, tar, and bash commands for managing files that are already compressed (such as zdiff, zcmp, zmore, and so forth).

The fourth section introduces you to the IFS option, which is useful for extracting data from a range of columns in a dataset. You will also see how to use the xargs command in order to "line up" the columns of a dataset so that all rows have the same number of columns.

The fifth section shows you how to create shell scripts, which contain bash commands that are executed sequentially, and also how to use recursion in order to compute the factorial value of a positive integer. The Appendix for this book contains additional shell scripts that use recursion in order to calculate the GCD (greatest common divisor) and LCM (lowest common multiple) of two positive integers, the Fibonacci value of a positive integer, and also the prime divisors of a positive integer.

The join Command

The join command allows you to merge two files in a meaningful fashion, which essentially creates a simple version of a relational database.

The join command operates on exactly two files, but pastes together only those lines with a common tagged field (usually a numerical label), and writes the result to stdout. The files to be joined should be sorted according to the tagged field for the matchups to work properly. Listing 2.1 and Listing 2.2 display the contents of 1.data and 2.data, respectively.

LISTING 2.1 1.data

```
100 Shoes
200 Laces
300 Socks
```

LISTING 2.2 2.data

```
100 $40.00
200 $1.00
300 $2.00
```

Now launch the following command:

```
join 1.data 2.data
```

The output is here:

1)   100 Shoes $40.00
2)   200 Laces $1.00
3)   300 Socks $2.00

The `fold` Command

As you know from Chapter 1, the `fold` command enables you to display a set of lines with a fixed column width, and this section contains a few more examples. Note that this command does not take into account spaces between words: the output is displayed in columns that resemble a "newspaper" style.

The following command displays a set of lines with ten characters in each line:

```
x="aa bb cc d e f g h i j kk ll mm nn"
echo $x |fold -10
```

The output of the preceding code snippet is here:

```
aa bb cc d
 e f g h i
 j kk ll m
m nn
```

As another example, consider the following code snippet:

```
x="The quick brown fox jumps over the fat lazy dog. "
echo $x |fold -10
```

The output of the preceding code snippet is here:

```
The quick
brown fox
jumps over
 the fat l
azy dog.
```

The `split` Command

The `split` command is useful when you want to create a set of subfiles of a given file. By default, the subfiles are named `xaa`, `xab`, . . ., `xaz`, `xba`, `xbb`, . . ., `xbz`, . . . `xza`, `xzb`, . . ., `xzz`. Thus, the `split` command creates a maximum of 676 files (=26x26). The default size for each of these files is 1,000 lines.

The following snippet illustrates how to invoke the `split` command in order to split the file `abc.txt` into files with 500 lines each:

```
split -l 500 one-dl-course-outline.txt
```

If the file `abc.txt` contains between 501 and 1,000 lines, then the preceding command will create the following pair of files:

```
xaa
xab
```

You can also specify a file prefix for the created files, as shown here:

```
split -l 500 one-dl-course-outline.txt shorter
```

The preceding command creates the following pair of files:

```
shorterxaa
shorterxab
```

The sort Command

The `sort` command sorts the lines in a text file. For example, if the text file `test2.txt` contains the following lines:

```
aa
cc
bb
```

The following simple example sorts the lines in `test2.txt`:

```
cat test2.txt |sort
```

The output of the preceding code snippet is here:

```
aa
bb
cc
```

The `sort` command arranges lines of text alphabetically by default. Some options for the `sort` command are here:

```
Option  Description
-n      Sort numerically (example: 10 will sort after 2),
ignore blanks and tabs.
-r      Reverse the order of sort.
-f      Sort upper- and lowercase together.
+x      Ignore first x fields when sorting.
```

You can use the `sort` command to display the files in a directory based on their file size, as shown here:

```
-rw-r--r--  1 ocampesato staff  11 Jan 06 19:21 outfile.txt
-rw-r--r--  1 ocampesato staff  12 Jan 06 19:21 output.txt
```

```
-rwx------  1 ocampesato staff   12 Jan 06 19:21 kyrgyzstan.txt
-rwx------  1 ocampesato staff   25 Jan 06 19:21 apple-care.txt
-rwx------  1 ocampesato staff  146 Jan 06 19:21 checkin-commands.txt
-rwx------  1 ocampesato staff  176 Jan 06 19:21 ssl-instructions.txt
-rwx------  1 ocampesato staff  417 Jan 06 19:43 iphonemeetup.txt
```

The `sort` command supports many options, some of which are summarized here.

The `sort` `-r` command sorts the list of files in reverse chronological order. The `sort` `-n` command sorts on numeric data and `sort` `-k` command sorts on a field. For example, the following command displays the long listing of the files in a directory that are sorted by their file size:

```
ls -l |sort -k 5
```

The output is here:

```
total 72
-rwx------  1 ocampesato staff   12 Jan 06 20:46 kyrgyzstan.txt
-rw-r--r--  1 ocampesato staff   12 Jan 06 20:46 output.txt
-rw-r--r--  1 ocampesato staff   14 Jan 06 20:46 outfile.txt
-rwx------  1 ocampesato staff   25 Jan 06 20:46 apple-care.txt
-rwxr-xr-x  1 ocampesato staff   90 Jan 06 20:50 testvars.sh
-rwxr-xr-x  1 ocampesato staff  100 Jan 06 20:50 testvars2.sh
-rwx------  1 ocampesato staff  146 Jan 06 20:46 checkin-commands.txt
-rwx------  1 ocampesato staff  176 Jan 06 20:46 ssl-instructions.txt
-rwx------  1 ocampesato staff  417 Jan 06 20:46 iphonemeetup.txt
```

Notice that the file listing is sorted based on the fifth column, which displays the file size of each file. You can sort the files in a directory and display them from largest to smallest with this command:

```
ls -l |sort -n
```

In addition to sorting lists of files, you can use the `sort` command to sort the contents of a file. For example, suppose that the file `abc2.txt` contains the following:

```
This is line one
This is line two
This is line one
This is line three
Fourth line
Fifth line
The sixth line
The seventh line
```

The following command sorts the contents of abc2.txt:

```
sort abc2.txt
```

You can sort the contents of multiple files and redirect the output to another file:

```
sort outfile.txt output.txt > sortedfile.txt
```

An example of combining the commands sort and tail is shown here:

```
cat abc2.txt |sort |tail -5
```

The preceding command sorts the contents of the file abc2.txt and then displays the final five lines:

```
The seventh line
The sixth line
This is line one
This is line one
This is line three
This is line two
```

As you can see, the preceding output contains two duplicate lines. The next section shows you how to use the uniq command in order to remove duplicate lines.

The uniq Command

The uniq command prints only the unique lines in a sorted text file and omits duplicates. As a simple example, suppose the file test3.txt contains the following lines:

```
abc
def
abc
abc
```

The following command displays the unique lines:

```
cat test3.txt |sort | uniq
```

The output of the preceding code snippet is here:

```
abc
def
```

How to Compare Files

The `diff` command enables you to compare two text files and the `cmp` command compares two binary files. For example, suppose that the file `output.txt` contains these two lines:

```
Hello
World
```

Suppose that the file `outfile.txt` contains these two lines:

```
goodbye
world
```

Then the output of this command:

```
diff output.txt outfile.txt
```

is shown here:

```
1,2c1,2
< Hello
< World
---
> goodbye
> world
```

Note that the `diff` command performs a case-sensitive text-based comparison, which means that the strings `Hello` and `hello` are different.

The od Command

The `od` command displays an octal dump of a file, which can be very helpful when you want to see embedded control characters (such as tab characters) that are not normally visible on the screen. This command contains many switches that you can see when you type `man od`.

As a simple example, suppose that the file `abc.txt` contains one line of text with the following three letters, separated by a tab character (which are not visible here) between each pair of letters:

```
a       b       c
```

The following command displays the tab and newline characters in the file `abc.txt`:

```
cat control1.txt |od -tc
```

The preceding command generates the following output:

```
0000000    a  \t    b  \t    c  \n
0000006
```

In the special case of tabs, another way to see them is to use the following cat command:

```
cat -t abc.txt
```

The output from the preceding command is here:

```
a^Ib^Ic
```

In Chapter 1 you learned that the echo command prints a newline character whereas the printf statement does not print a newline character (unless it is explicitly included). You can verify this fact for yourself with this code snippet:

```
echo abcde | od -c
0000000    a    b    c    d    e    \n
0000006
printf abcde | od -c
0000000    a    b    c    d    e
0000005
```

The tr Command

The tr command is a highly versatile command that supports many operations. For example, the tr command enables you to remove extraneous whitespaces in datasets, insert blank lines, print words on separate lines, and also translate characters from one character set to another character set (i.e., from uppercase to lowercase, and vice versa).

The following command capitalizes the letters in the variable x:

```
x="abc def ghi"
echo $x | tr [a-z] [A-Z]
ABC DEF GHI
```

Another way to convert from lowercase to uppercase:

```
cat columns4.txt   |   tr '[:lower:]' '[:upper:]'
```

In addition to upper and lower, you can use the POSIX character classes in the tr command:

alnum: alphanumeric characters
alpha: alphabetic characters
cntrl: control (non-printing) characters
digit: numeric characters
graph: graphic characters
lower: lowercase alphabetic characters
print: printable characters
punct: punctuation characters
space: whitespace characters
upper: uppercase characters
xdigit: hexadecimal characters 0–9 A–F

The following example removes white spaces in the variable x (initialized above):

```
echo $x |tr -ds " " ""
abcdefghi
```

The following command prints each word on a separate line:

```
echo "a b c" | tr -s " " "\012"
a
b
c
```

The following command replaces commas "," with a linefeed:

```
echo "a,b,c" | tr -s "," "\n"
a
b
c
```

The following example replaces the linefeed in each line with a blank space, which produces a single line of output:

```
cat test4.txt |tr '\n' ' '
```

The output of the preceding command is here:

```
abc  def  abc  abc
```

The following example removes the linefeed character at the end of each line of text in a text file. As an illustration, Listing 2.3 displays the contents of abc2.txt.

LISTING 2.3 abc2.txt

```
This is line one
This is line two
This is line three
Fourth line
Fifth line
The sixth line
The seventh line
```

The following code snippet removes the linefeed character in the text file abc2.txt:

```
tr -d '\n' < abc2.txt
```

The output of the preceding `tr` code snippet is here:

```
This is line oneThis is line twoThis is line threeFourth line-
Fifth lineThe sixth lineThe seventh line
```

As you can see, the output is missing a blank space between consecutive lines, which we can insert with this command:

```
tr -s '\n' ' ' < abc2.txt
```

The output of the modified version of the `tr` code snippet is here:

```
This is line one This is line two This is line three Fourth line
Fifth line The sixth line The seventh line
```

You can replace the linefeed character with a period "." with this version of the `tr` command:

```
tr -s '\n' '.' < abc2.txt
```

The output of the preceding version of the `tr` code snippet is here:

```
This is line one.This is line two.This is line three.Fourth
line.Fifth line.The sixth line.The seventh line.
```

The `tr` command with the `-s` option works on a one-for-one basis, which means that the sequence "." has the same effect as the sequence ". ". As a sort of "preview," we can add a blank space after each period "." by combining the `tr` command with the `sed` command (discussed in Chapter 4), as shown here:

```
tr -s '\n' '.' < abc2.txt | sed 's/\./\. /g'
```

The output of the preceding command is here:

```
This is line one. This is line two. This is line three. Fourth
line. Fifth line. The sixth line. The seventh line.
```

Think of the preceding sed snippet as follows: "whenever a 'dot' is encountered, replace it with a 'dot' followed by a space, and do this for every such occurrence."

You can also combine multiple commands using the Unix pipe symbol. For example, the following command sorts the contents of Listing 2.3, retrieves the "bottom" five lines of text, retrieves the lines of text that are unique, and then converts the text to upper case letters,

```
cat abc2.txt  |sort |tail -5 | uniq | tr [a-z] [A-Z]
```

Here is the output from the preceding command

```
THE SEVENTH LINE
THE SIXTH LINE
THIS IS LINE ONE
THIS IS LINE THREE
THIS IS LINE TWO
```

You can also convert the first letter of a word to uppercase (or to lowercase) with the tr command, as shown here:

```
x="pizza"
x=`echo ${x:0:1} | tr  '[a-z]' '[A-Z]'`${x:1}
echo $x
```

A slightly longer (one extra line of code) way to convert the first letter to uppercase is shown here:

```
x="pizza"
first=`echo $x|cut -c1|tr [a-z] [A-Z]`
second=`echo $x|cut -c2-`
echo $first$second
```

However, both of the preceding code blocks are somewhat obscure (at least for novices), so it's probably better to use other tools, such as dataframes in R or RStudio.

As you can see, it's possible to combine multiple commands using the bash pipe symbol "|" in order to produce the desired output.

A Simple Use Case

The code sample in this section shows you how to use the `tr` command in order to replace the control character "^M" with a linefeed. Listing 2.4 displays the contents of the dataset `controlm.csv` that contains embedded control characters.

LISTING 2.4 controlm.csv

```
IDN,TEST,WEEK_MINUS1,WEEK0,WEEK1,WEEK2,WEEK3,WEEK4,WEEK10,WEEK
12,WEEK14,WEEK15,WEEK17,WEEK18,WEEK19,
WEEK21^M1,BASO,,1.4,,0.8,,1.2,,1.1,,,2.2,,,1.4^M1,
BASOAB,,0.05,,0.04,,0.05,,0.04,,,0.07,,,0.05^M1,EOS,,
6.1,,6.2,,7.5,,6.6,,,7.0,,,6.2^M1,EOSAB,,0.22,,0.30,,
0.27,,0.25,,,0.22,,,0.21^M1,HCT,,35.0,,34.2,,34.6,,34.3,,,36.2
,,,34.1^M1,HGB,,11.8,,11.1,,11.6,,11.5,,,12.1,,,
11.3^M1,LYM,,36.7
```

Listing 2.5 displays the contents of the file `controlm.sh` that illustrates how to remove the control characters from `controlm.csv`.

LISTING 2.5 controlm.sh

```
inputfile="controlm.csv"
removectrlmfile="removectrlmfile"
tr -s '\r' '\n' < $inputfile > $removectrlmfile
```

For convenience, Listing 2.5 contains a variable for the input file and one for the output file, but you can simplify the `tr` command in Listing 2.5 by using hard-coded values for the filenames.

The output from launching the shell script in Listing 2.5 is here:

```
IDN,TEST,WEEK_MINUS1,WEEK0,WEEK1,WEEK2,WEEK3,WEEK4,WEEK10,WEEK
12,WEEK14,WEEK15,WEEK17,WEEK18,WEEK19,WEEK21
1,BASO,,1.4,,0.8,,1.2,,1.1,,,2.2,,,1.4
1,BASOAB,,0.05,,0.04,,0.05,,0.04,,,0.07,,,0.05
1,EOS,,6.1,,6.2,,7.5,,6.6,,,7.0,,,6.2
1,EOSAB,,0.22,,0.30,,0.27,,0.25,,,0.22,,,0.21
```

As you can see, the task in this section is very easily solved via the `tr` command. Note that additional data cleaning is required in order to handle the empty fields in the output.

You can also replace the current delimiter "," with a different delimiter, such as a "|" symbol with the following command:

```
cat removectrlmfile |tr -s ',' '|' > pipedfile
```

The resulting output is shown here:

```
IDN|TEST|WEEK_MINUS1|WEEK0|WEEK1|WEEK2|WEEK3|WEEK4|WEEK10|WEEK
12|WEEK14|WEEK15|WEEK17|WEEK18|WEEK19|WEEK21
1|BASO|1.4|0.8|1.2|1.1|2.2|1.4
1|BASOAB|0.05|0.04|0.05|0.04|0.07|0.05
1|EOS|6.1|6.2|7.5|6.6|7.0|6.2
1|EOSAB|0.22|0.30|0.27|0.25|0.22|0.21
```

If you have a dataset with multiple delimiters in arbitrary order in multiple files, you can replace those delimiters with a single delimiter via the sed command, which is discussed in Chapter 4.

The find Command

The find command supports many options, including one for printing (displaying) the files returned by the find command, and another one for removing the files returned by the find command.

In addition, you can specify logical operators such as AND as well as OR in a find command. You can also specify switches to find the files (if any) that were created, accessed, or modified before (or after) a specific date.

Several examples are here:

find . -print displays all the files (including subdirectories)
find . -print |grep "abc" displays all the files whose names contain the string abc
find . -print |grep "sh$" displays all the files whose names have the suffix sh
find . -depth 2 -print displays all files of depth at most 2 (including subdirectories)

You can also specify access times pertaining to files. For example, atime, ctime, and mtime refer to the access time, creation time, and modification time of a file.

As another example, the following command finds all the files modified in less than 2 days and prints the record count of each:

```
$ find . -mtime -2 -exec wc -l {} ;
```

You can remove a set of files with the find command. For example, you can remove all the files in the current directory tree that have the suffix "m" as follows:

```
find . -name "*m$" -print -exec rm {}
```

NOTE *Be careful when you remove files: run the preceding command without* `"exec rm {}"` *to review the list of files before deleting them.*

The tee Command

The tee command enables you to display output to the screen and also redirect the output to a file at the same time. The -a option will append subsequent output to the named file instead of overwriting the file. An example is here:

```
find . -print |xargs grep "sh$" | tee /tmp/blue
```

The preceding code snippet redirects the list of all files in the current directory (and those in any subdirectories) to the xargs command, which then searches—and prints—all the lines that end with the string "sh." The result is displayed on the screen and is also redirected to the file /tmp/blue.

```
find . -print |xargs grep "^abc$" | tee -a /tmp/blue
```

The preceding code snippet also redirects the list of all files in the current directory (and those in any subdirectories) to the xargs command, which then searches—and prints—all the lines that contain only the string "abc." The result is displayed on the screen and is also *appended* to the file /tmp/blue.

File Compression Commands

Bash supports various commands for compressing sets of files, including the tar, cpio, gzip, and gunzip commands. The following subsections contain simple examples of how to use these commands.

The tar Command

The tar command enables you to compress a set of files in a directory, uncompress a tar file, and also display the contents of a tar file.

The "c" option specifies "create," the "f" option specifies "file," and the "v" option specifies "verbose." For example, the following command creates a compressed file called testing.tar and displays the files that are included in `testing.tar` during the creation of this file:

```
tar cvf testing.tar *.txt
```

The compressed file `testing.tar` contains the files with the suffix txt in the current directory, and you will see the following output:

```
a apple-care.txt
a checkin-commands.txt
a iphonemeetup.txt
a kyrgyzstan.txt
a outfile.txt
a output.txt
a ssl-instructions.txt
```

The following command extracts the files that are in the tar file testing. tar:

```
tar xvf testing.tar
```

The following command displays the contents of a tar file without uncompressing its contents:

```
tar tvf testing.tar
```

The preceding command displays the same output as the "ls -l" command that displays a long listing.

The "z" option uses `gzip` compression. For example, the following command creates a compressed file called `testing.tar.gz`:

```
tar czvf testing.tar.gz *.txt
```

The cpio Command

The cpio command provides further compression after you create a tar file. For example, the following command creates the file `archive.cpio`:

```
ls file1 file2 file3 | cpio -ov > archive.cpio
```

The "-o" option specifies an output file and the "-v" option specifies verbose, which means that the files are displayed as they are placed in the archive file. The "-I" option specifies input, and the "-d" option specifies "display."

You can combine other commands (such as the find command) with the cpio command, an example of which is here:

```
find . -name ".sh" | cpio -ov > shell-scripts.cpio
```

You can display the contents of the file archive.cpio with the following command:

```
cpio -id < archive.cpio
```

The output of the preceding command is here:

```
file1
file2
file3
1 block
```

The gzip and gunzip Commands

The gzip command creates a compressed file. For example, the following command creates the compressed file filename.gz:

```
gzip filename
```

Extract the contents of the compressed file filename.gz with the gunzip command:

```
gunzip filename.gz
```

You can create gzipped tarballs using the following methods:

Method #1:

```
tar -czvf archive.tar.gz [LIST-OF-FILES]
```

Method #2:

```
tar -cavf  archive.tar.gz [LIST-OF-FILES]
```

The -a option specifies that the compression format should automatically be detected from the extension.

The bunzip2 Command

The bunzip2 utility uses a compression technique that is similar to gunzip2, except that bunzip2 typically produces smaller (more compressed) files than `gzip`. It comes with all Linux distributions. In order to compress with `bzip2` use:

```
bzip2 filename
ls
filename.bz2
```

The `zip` Command

The `zip` command is another utility for creating zip files. For example, if you have the files called `file1`, `file2`, and `file3`, then the following command creates the file `file1.zip` that contains these three files:

```
zip file?
```

The `zip` command has useful options (such as `-x` for excluding files), and you can find more information in online tutorials.

Commands for `zip` Files and `bz` Files

There are various commands for handling `zip` files, including `zdiff`, `zcmp`, `zmore`, `zless`, `zcat`, `zipgrep`, `zipsplit`, `zipinfo`, `zgrep`, `zfgrep`, and `zegrep`.

Remove the initial "z" or "zip" from these commands to obtain the corresponding "regular" `bash` command.

For example, the `zcat` command is the counterpart to the `cat` command, so you can display the contents of a file in a `.gz` file without manually extracting that file and also without modifying the contents of the `.gz` file. Here is an example:

```
ls test.gz
zcat test.gz
```

A test file

file test contains a line "A test file"

Another set of utilities for `bz` files includes `bzcat`, `bzcmp`, `bzdiff`, `bzegrep`, `bzfgrep`, `bzgrep`, `bzless`, and `bzmore`.
Read the online documentation to find out more about these commands.

Internal Field Separator (IFS)

The Internal Field Separator is an important concept in shell script-ing that is useful while manipulating text data. An Internal Field Separator (IFS) is an environment variable that stores delimiting characters. The IFS is the default delimiter string used by a running shell environment.

Consider the case where we need to iterate through words in a string or comma separated values (CSV). In the first case we will use IFS=" " and in the second we will use IFS=",". Suppose that the shell variable data is defined as follows:

```
data="name,sex,rollno,location"
```

#To read each of the data elements into a variable, we can use IFS as shown here:

```
oldIFS=$IFS
IFS=,
for item in `echo $data`
do
   echo Item: $item
done
IFS=$oldIFS
```

The next section contains a code sample that relies on the value of IFS in order to extract data correctly from a dataset.

Data from a Range of Columns in a Dataset

Listing 2.6 displays the contents of the dataset datacolumns1.txt and Listing 2.7 displays the contents of the shell script datacolumns1.sh that illustrates how to extract data from a range of columns from the data-set in Listing 2.6.

LISTING 2.6 datacolumns1.txt

```
#234567890123456789012345678990
   1000    Jane      Edwards
   2000    Tom       Smith
   3000    Dave      Del Ray
```

LISTING 2.7 datacolumns1.sh

```
# empid: 03-09
# fname: 11-20
# lname: 21-30
IFS=''
inputfile="datacolumns1.txt"

while read line
do
  pound="`echo $line |grep '^#'`"

  if [ x"$pound" == x"" ]
  then
    echo "line: $line"
    empid=`echo "$line" |cut -c3-9`
    echo "empid: $empid"

    fname=`echo "$line" |cut -c11-19`
    echo "fname: $fname"

    lname=`echo "$line" |cut -c21-29`
    echo "lname: $lname"
    echo "-------------"
  fi
done < $inputfile
```

Listing 2.7 sets the value of IFS to an empty string, which is required for this shell script to work correctly (try running this script without setting IFS and see what happens). The body of this script contains a while loop that reads each line from the input file called datacolumns1.txt and sets the pound variable equal to "" if a line does not start with the "#" character OR sets the pound variable equal to the entire line if it *does* start with the "#" character. This is a simple technique for "filtering" lines based on their initial character.

The if statement executes for lines that do not start with a "#" character, and the variables empid, fname, and lname are initialized to the characters in columns 3 through 9, then 11 through 19, and then 21 through 29, respectively. The values of those three variables are printed each time they are initialized. As you can see, these variables are initialized by a combination of the echo command and the cut command, and the value of IFS is required in order to ensure that the echo command does not remove blank spaces.

The output from Listing 2.7 is shown below:

```
line:    1000    Jane       Edwards
empid: 1000
fname: Jane
lname: Edwards
--------------
line:    2000    Tom        Smith
empid: 2000
fname: Tom
lname: Smith
--------------
line:    3000    Dave       Del Ray
empid: 3000
fname: Dave
lname: Del Ray
--------------
```

Working with Uneven Rows in Datasets

Listing 2.8 displays the contents of the dataset uneven.txt that contains rows with a different number of columns. Listing 2.9 displays the contents of the bash script uneven.sh that illustrates how to generate a dataset whose rows have the same number of columns.

LISTING 2.8 uneven.txt

```
abc1 abc2 abc3 abc4
abc5 abc6
abc1 abc2 abc3 abc4
abc5 abc6
```

LISTING 2.9 uneven.sh

```
inputfile="uneven.txt"
outputfile="even2.txt"

# ==> four fields per line

#method #1: four fields per line
cat $inputfile | xargs -n 4 >$outputfile

#method #2: two equal rows
#xargs -L 2 <$inputfile > $outputfile

echo "input file:"
cat $inputfile
```

```
echo "output file:"
cat $outputfile
```

Listing 2.9 contains two techniques for realigning the input file so that the output appears with four columns in each row. As you can see, both techniques involve the `xargs` command (which is an interesting use of the `xargs` command).

Launch the code in Listing 2.9 and you will see the following output:

```
abc1 abc2 abc3 abc4
abc5 abc6 abc1 abc2
abc3 abc4 abc5 abc6
```

Working with Functions in Shell Scripts

A shell function can be defined by using the keyword `function`, followed by the name of the function (specified by you) and a pair of round parentheses, followed by a pair of curly braces that contain shell commands. The general form is shown here:

```
function fname()
{
    statements;
}
```

An alternate method of defining a shell function is shown here:

```
fname()
{
    statements;
}
```

A function can be invoked by its name:

```
fname ; # executes function
```

Arguments can be passed to functions and can be accessed by the shell script:

```
fname arg1 arg2 ; # passing args
```

Listing 2.10 displays the contents of `checkuser.sh`, which illustrates how to prompt users for two input strings and then invoke a function with those strings as parameters.

LISTING 2.10 checkuser.sh

```bash
#!/bin/bash

function checkNewUser()
{
  echo "argument #1 = $1"
  echo "argument #2 = $2"
  echo "arg count   = $#"

  if test "$1" = "John" && test "$2" = "Smith"
  then
    return 1
  else
    return 0
  fi
}

/bin/echo -n "First name: "
read fname
/bin/echo -n "Last name: "
read lname

checkNewUser $fname $lname
echo "result = $?"
```

Listing 2.10 contains the function checkNewUser() that displays the value of the first argument, the second argument, and the total number of arguments, respectively. This function returns the value 1 if the first argument is John and the second argument is Smith; otherwise the function returns 0.

The remaining portion of Listing 2.10 invokes the echo command twice in order to prompt users to enter a first name and a last name, and then invokes the function checkNewUser() with these two input values. A sample output from launching Listing 2.10 is shown here:

```
First name: John
Last name: Smith
argument #1 = John
argument #2 = Smith
arg count   = 2
result = 1
```

What about using command substitution in order to invoke the function checkNewUser? In order to find out what would happen, let's add the following code snippet to the bottom of Listing 2.10:

```
result=`checkNewUser $fname $lname`
echo "result = $result"
```

Launch the modified version of Listing 2.10, provide the same input values of John and Smith, and compare the following result with the previous result:

```
First name: John
Last name: Smith
argument #1 = John
argument #2 = Smith
arg count   = 2
result = 1
result = argument #1 = John
argument #2 = Smith
arg count   = 2
```

Recursion and Shell Scripts

This section contains several examples of shell scripts with recursion, which is a topic that occurs in many programming languages. Although you probably won't need to write many scripts that use recursion, it's worthwhile to learn this concept, especially if you plan to study other languages.

If you already understand recursion, then the scripts in this section will be straightforward. In particular, you will learn how to calculate the factorial value of a positive integer. In case you are interested, the Appendix contains bash scripts for calculating the Fibonacci number of a positive integer, as well as bash scripts for calculating the greatest common divisor (GCD) and the least common multiple (LCM) of two positive integers.

Listing 2.11 displays the contents of Factorial.sh that computes the factorial value of a positive integer.

LISTING 2.11 Factorial.sh

```
#!/bin/sh

factorial()
{
    if [ "$1" -gt 1 ]
    then
        decr=`expr $1 - 1`
        result=`factorial $decr`
        product=`expr $1 \* $result`
        echo $product
    else
        # we have reached 1:
        echo 1
```

```
        fi
}
echo "Enter a number: "
read num

# add code to ensure it's a positive integer

echo "$num! = `factorial $num`"
```

Listing 2.11 contains the `factorial()` function with conditional logic: if the first parameter is greater than 1, then the variable `decr` is initialized as 1 less than the value of $1, followed by initializing result with the recursive invocation of the `factorial()` function with the argument `decr`. Finally, this block of code initializes product as the value of $1 multiplied by the value of result. Note that if the first parameter is not greater than 1, then the value 1 is returned.

The last portion of Listing 2.11 prompts users for a number and then the factorial value of that number is computed and displayed. For simplicity, non-integer values are not checked (you can try to add that functionality yourself).

Iterative Solutions for Factorial Values

Listing 2.12 displays the contents of `Factorial2.sh`, which computes the factorial value of a positive integer using a `for` loop.

LISTING 2.12 Factorial2.sh

```
#!/bin/bash

factorial()
{
    num=$1
    result=1
    for (( i=2; i<=${num}; i++ ));
    do
      result=$((${result}*$i))
    done

    echo $result
}

printf "Enter a number: "
read num

echo "$num! = `factorial $num`"
```

Listing 2.12 contains a function called `factorial()` that initializes the variable num to the first argument passed into the function `factorial()`, followed by the variable `result` whose initial value is 1. The next portion of Listing 2.12 is a `for` loop that iteratively multiples the value of result by the numbers between 2 and num inclusive, and then returns the value of the variable `result`.

The final portion of Listing 2.12 prompts users for a number and then uses command substitution to invoke the function `factorial()` with the user-supplied value. Note that no validation is performed in order to ensure that the input value is a non-negative integer. The `echo` statement displays the calculated factorial value.

Listing 2.13 displays the contents of `Factorial3.sh`, which computes the factorial value of a positive integer using a `for` loop and an array that keeps track of intermediate factorial values.

LISTING 2.13 Factorial3.sh

```
#!/bin/bash

factorial()
{
    num=$1
    result=1
    for (( i=2; i<=${num}; i++ ));
    do
      result=$((${result}*$i))
      factvalues[$i]=$result
    done
}

printf "Enter a number: "
read num

for (( i=1; i<=${num}; i++ ));
do
  factvalues[$i]=1
done

factorial $num

# print each element via a loop:
for (( i=1; i<=${num}; i++ ));
do
  echo "Factorial of $i : " ${factvalues[$i]}
done
```

Listing 2.13 is very similar to the code in Listing 2.12: the key difference is that intermediate factorial values are stored in the array factvalues. Notice that initial loop that initializes the values in factvalues: doing so makes the values global, so we don't need to return anything from the factorial() function.

The last portion of Listing 2.13 contains a for loop that displays the intermediate factorial values as well as the factorial of the user-provided input.

Summary

This chapter showed you examples of how to use some useful and versatile bash commands. First you learned about the bash commands join, fold, split, sort, and uniq. Next you learned about the find command and the xargs command. You also learned about various ways to use the tr command, which is also in the use case in this chapter.

Then you saw some compression-related commands, such as cpio and tar, which help you create new compressed files and also help you examine the contents of compressed files.

In addition, you learned how to extract column ranges of data, as well as the usefulness of the IFS option. Finally, you saw an example of a bash script for computing the factorial value of a number via recursion.

CHAPTER 3

FILTERING DATA WITH grep

This chapter introduces you to the versatile grep command, whose purpose is to take a stream of text data and reduce it to only the parts that you care about. The grep command is useful not only by itself, but also in conjunction with other commands, especially the find command. This chapter contains many short code samples that illustrate various options of the grep command. Some code samples illustrate how to combine the grep command with commands from previous chapters.

The first part of this chapter introduces the grep command used in isolation, combined with the regular expression metacharacters (from Chapter 1) and also with code snippets that illustrate how to use some of the options of the grep command. Next you will learn how to match ranges of lines, how to use the so-called "back references" in grep, and how to "escape" metacharacters in grep.

The second part of this chapter shows you how to use the grep command in order to find empty lines and common lines in datasets, as well as how to use keys to match rows in datasets. Next you will learn how to use character classes with the grep command, as well as the backslash "\" character, and how to specify multiple matching patterns. Next you will learn how to combine the grep command with the find command and the xargs command, which is useful for matching a pattern in files that reside in different directories. This section also contains some examples of common mistakes that people make with the grep command.

The third section briefly discusses the egrep command and the fgrep command, which are related commands that provide additional functionality that is unavailable in the standard grep utility. The final section contains a use case that illustrates how to use the grep command in order to find matching lines that are then merged in order to create a new dataset.

What Is the grep Command?

The grep ("Global Regular Expression Print") command is useful for finding substrings in one or more files. Several examples are here:

grep abc *sh displays all the *lines* of abc in files with suffix sh

grep -i abc *sh is the same as the preceding query, but case-insensitive

grep -l abc *sh displays all the *filenames* with suffix sh that contain abc

grep -n abc *sh displays all the *line numbers* of the occurrences of the string abc in files with suffix sh

You can perform logical AND and logical OR operations with this syntax:

grep abc *sh | grep def matches lines containing abc AND def

grep "abc\|def" *sh matches lines containing abc OR def

You can combine switches as well: the following command displays the names of the files that contain the string abc (case insensitive):

```
grep -il abc *sh
```

In other words, the preceding command matches filenames that contain abc, Abc, ABc, ABC, abC, and so forth.

Another (less efficient way) to display the lines containing abc (case insensitive) is here:

```
cat file1 |grep -i abc
```

The preceding command involves two processes, whereas the "grep using –l switch instead of cat to input the files you want" approach involves a single process. The execution time is roughly the same for small text files, but the execution time can become more significant if you are working with multiple large text files.

You can combine the sort command, the pipe symbol, and the grep command. For example, the following command displays the files with a "Jan" date in increasing size:

```
ls -l |grep " Jan " | sort -n
```

A sample output from the preceding command is here:

```
-rw-r--r-- 1 oswaldcampesato2 staff    3 Sep 27 2017 abc.txt
-rw-r--r-- 1 oswaldcampesato2 staff    6 Sep 21 2017 control1.txt
-rw-r--r-- 1 oswaldcampesato2 staff   27 Sep 28 2017 fiblist.txt
-rw-r--r-- 1 oswaldcampesato2 staff   28 Sep 14 2017 dest
-rw-r--r-- 1 oswaldcampesato2 staff   36 Sep 14 2017 source
-rw-r--r-- 1 oswaldcampesato2 staff  195 Sep 28 2017 Divisors.py
-rw-r--r-- 1 oswaldcampesato2 staff  267 Sep 28 2017 Divisors2.py
```

Metacharacters and the `grep` Command

The fundamental building blocks are the regular expressions that match a single character. Most characters, including all letters and digits, are regular expressions that match themselves. Any meta-character with special meaning may be quoted by preceding it with a backslash.

A regular expression may be followed by one of several repetition operators, as shown below.

'.' matches any single character.

'?' indicates that the preceding item is optional and will be matched at most once: Z? matches Z or ZZ.

'*' indicates that the preceding item will be matched zero or more times: Z* matches Z, ZZ, ZZZ, and so forth.

'+' indicates that the preceding item will be matched one or more times: Z+ matches ZZ, ZZZ, and so forth.

'{n}'indicates that the preceding item is matched exactly n times: Z{3} matches ZZZ.

'{n,}' indicates that the preceding item is matched n or more times: Z{3} matches ZZZ, ZZZZ, and so forth.

'{,m}' indicates that the preceding item is matched at most m times: Z{,3} matches Z, ZZ, and ZZZ.

'{n,m}' indicates that the preceding item is matched at least n times, but not more than m times: Z{2,4} matches ZZ, ZZZ, and ZZZZ.

The empty regular expression matches the empty string (i.e., a line in the input stream with no data). Two regular expressions may be joined by the infix operator '|.' When used in this manner, the infix operator behaves exactly like a logical "OR" statement, which directs the `grep` command to return any line that matches either regular expression.

Escaping Metacharacters with the `grep` Command

Listing 3.1 displays the contents of `lines.txt`, which contains lines with words and metacharacters.

LISTING 3.1 *lines.txt*

```
abcd
ab
abc
cd
defg
.*.
..
```

The following `grep` command lists the lines of length 2 (using the ^ begin with and $ end with operators to restrict length) in `lines.txt`:

```
grep '^..$' lines.txt
```

The following command lists the lines of length two in `lines.txt` that contain two dots (the backslash tells `grep` to interpret the dots as actual dots, not as metacharacters):

```
grep '^\.\.$' lines.txt
```

The result is shown here:

```
ab
cd
..
```

The following command also displays lines of length two that begin and end with a dot (the * matches any text of any length, including no text at all, and is used as a metacharacter because it is not preceded with a backslash):

```
grep '^.*.$' lines.txt
```

The following command lists the lines that contain a period, followed by an asterisk, and then another period (the * is now a character that must be matched because it is preceded by a backslash):

```
grep '^\.\*\.$' lines.txt
```

Useful Options for the `grep` Command

There are many types of pattern matching possibilities with the `grep` command, and this section contains an eclectic mix of such commands that handle common scenarios.

In the following examples we have four text files (two .sh and two .txt) and two Word documents in a directory. The string `abc` is found on one line in `abc1.txt` and three lines in `abc3.sh`. The string `ABC` is found on 2 lines in in `ABC2.txt` and 4 lines in `ABC4.sh`. Notice that `abc` is not found in `ABC` files, and `ABC` is not found in `abc` files.

```
ls *
ABC.doc    ABC4.sh         abc1.txt       ABC2.txt   abc.doc
abc3.sh
```

The following code snippet searches for occurrences of the string `abc` in all the files in the current directory that have `sh` as a suffix:

```
grep abc *sh
abc3.sh:abc at start
abc3.sh:ends with -abc
abc3.sh:the abc is in the middle
```

The "-c" option counts the number of occurrences of a string (note that even though `ABC4.sh` has no matches, it still counts them and returns zero):

```
grep -c abc *sh
```

The output of the preceding command is here:

```
ABC4.sh:0
abc3.sh:3
```

The "-e" option lets you match patterns that would otherwise cause syntax problems (the "-" character normally is interpreted as an argument for `grep`):

```
grep -e "-abc" *sh
abc3.sh:ends with -abc
```

The "-e" option also lets you match multiple patterns.

```
grep -e "-abc" -e "comment" *sh
ABC4.sh:# ABC in a comment
abc3.sh:ends with -abc
```

The "-i" option is to perform a case insensitive match:

```
grep -i abc *sh
ABC4.sh:ABC at start
ABC4.sh:ends with ABC
ABC4.sh:the ABC is in the middle
ABC4.sh:# ABC in a comment
abc3.sh:abc at start
abc3.sh:ends with -abc
abc3.sh:the abc is in the middle
```

The "-v" option "inverts" the matching string, which means that the output consists of the lines that do not contain the specified string (ABC doesn't match because -i is not used, and ABC4.sh has an entirely empty line):

```
grep -v abc *sh
```

Use the "-iv" options to display the lines that do not contain a specified string using a case insensitive match:

```
grep -iv abc *sh
ABC4.sh:
abc3.sh:this line won't match
```

The "-l" option is to list only the filenames that contain a successful match (note this matches contents of files, not the filenames). The Word document matches because the actual text is still visible to grep, it is just surrounded by proprietary formatting gibberish. You can do similar things with other formats that contain text, such as XML, HTML, .csv, and so forth:

```
grep -l abc *
abc1.txt
abc3.sh
abc.doc
```

The "-l" option is to list only the filenames that contain a successful match:

```
grep -l abc *sh
```

Use the "-il" options to display the filenames that contain a specified string using a case insensitive match:

```
grep -il abc *doc
```

The preceding command is very useful when you want to check for the occurrence of a string in Word documents.

The "-n" option specifies line numbers of any matching file:

```
grep -n abc *sh
abc3.sh:1:abc at start
abc3.sh:2:ends with -abc
abc3.sh:3:the abc is in the middle
```

The "-h" option suppresses the display of the filename for a successful match:

```
grep -h abc *sh
abc at start
ends with -abc
the abc is in the middle
```

For the next series of examples, we will use `columns4.txt` as shown in Listing 3.2.

LISTING 3.2 columns4.txt

```
123 ONE TWO
456 three four
ONE TWO THREE FOUR
five 123 six
one two three
    four five
```

The "-o" option shows only the matched string (this is how you avoid returning the entire line that matches):

```
grep -o one columns4.txt
```

The "-o" option followed by the "-b" option shows the position of the matched string (returns character position, not line number. The "o" in "one" is the 59th character of the file):

```
grep -o -b one columns4.txt
```

You can specify a recursive search as shown here (output not shown because it will be different on every client or account. This searches not only every file in directory /etc, but every file in every subdirectory of etc):

```
grep -r abc /etc
```

The preceding commands match lines where the specified string is a substring of a longer string in the file. For instance, the preceding commands will match occurrences of abc as well as abcd, dabc, abcde, and so forth.

```
grep ABC *txt
ABC2.txt:ABC at start or ABC in middle or end in ABC
ABC2.txt:ABCD DABC
```

If you want to exclude everything except for an exact match, you can use the -w option, as shown here:

```
grep -w ABC *txt
ABC2.txt:ABC at start or ABC in middle or end in ABC
```

The --color switch displays the matching string in color:

```
grep --color abc *sh
abc3.sh:abc at start
abc3.sh:ends with -abc
abc3.sh:the abc is in the middle
```

You can use the pair of metacharacters .* to find the occurrences of two words that are separated by an arbitrary number of intermediate characters.

The following command finds all lines that contain the strings one and three with any number of intermediate characters:

```
grep "one.*three" columns4.txt
one two three
```

You can "invert" the preceding result by using the -v switch, as shown here:

```
grep -v "one.*three" columns4.txt
123 ONE TWO
456 three four
ONE TWO THREE FOUR
five 123 six
four five
```

The following command finds all lines that contain the strin gs one and three with any number of intermediate characters, where the match involves a case-insensitive comparison:

```
grep -i "one.*three" columns4.txt
ONE TWO THREE FOUR
one two three
```

You can "invert" the preceding result by using the -v switch, as shown here:

```
grep -iv "one.*three" columns4.txt
123 ONE TWO
456 three four
five 123 six
four five
```

Sometimes you need to search a file for the presence of either of two strings. For example, the following command finds the files that contain "start" or "end":

```
grep -l 'start\|end' *
ABC2.txt
ABC4.sh
abc3.sh
```

Later in the chapter you will see how to find files that contain a pair of strings via the grep and xargs commands.

Character Classes and the grep Command

This section contains some simple one-line commands that combine the grep command with character classes.

```
echo "abc" | grep '[:alpha:]'
abc
echo "123" | grep '[:alpha:]'
(returns nothing, no match)
echo "abc123" | grep '[:alpha:]'
abc123
echo "abc" | grep '[:alnum:]'
abc
echo "123" | grep '[:alnum:]'
(returns nothing, no match)
echo "abc123" | grep '[:alnum:]'
abc123
echo "123" | grep '[:alnum:]'
(returns nothing, no match)
echo "abc123" | grep '[:alnum:]'
abc123
echo "abc" | grep '[0-9]'
(returns nothing, no match)
echo "123" | grep '[0-9]'
123
echo "abc123" | grep '[0-9]'
abc123
echo "abc123" | grep -w '[0-9]'
(returns nothing, no match)
```

Working with the −c Option in grep

Consider a scenario in which a directory (such as a log directory) has files created by an outside program. Your task is to write a shell script that determines which (if any) of the files that contain two occurrences of a string, after which additional processing is performed on the matching files (e.g., use email to send log files containing two or more error messages to a system administrator for investigation).

One solution involves the −c option for grep, followed by additional invocations of the grep command.

The command snippets in this section assume the following data files whose contents are shown below.

The file hello1.txt contains the following:

```
hello world1
```

The file hello2.txt contains the following:

```
hello world2
hello world2 second time
```

The file hello3.txt contains the following:

```
hello world3
hello world3 two
hello world3 three
```

Now launch the following commands: (2>/dev/null keeps warnings and errors caused by empty directories from cluttering up the output):

```
grep -c hello hello*txt 2>/dev/null
hello1.txt:1
hello2.txt:2
hello3.txt:3
grep -l hello hello*txt 2>/dev/null
hello1.txt
hello2.txt
hello3.txt
grep -c hello hello*txt 2>/dev/null |grep ":2$"
hello2.txt:2
```

Note how we use the "ends with" "$" metacharacter to grab just the files that have exactly two matches. We also use the colon ":2$" rather than just "2$" to prevent grabbing files that have 12, 32, or 142 matches (which would end in :12, :32, and :142).

What if we wanted to show "two or more" (as in the "2 or more errors in a log")? You would instead use the invert (-v) command to exclude counts of exactly 0 or exactly 1.

```
grep -c hello hello*txt 2>/dev/null |grep -v ':[0-1]$'
hello2.txt:2
hello3.txt:3
```

In a real-world application, you would want to strip off everything after the colon to return only the filenames. There are many ways to do so, but we'll use the cut command we learned in Chapter 1, which involves defining : as a delimiter with -d":" and using -f1 to return the first column (i.e., the part before the colon in the return text):

```
grep -c hello hello*txt 2>/dev/null | grep -v ':[0-1]$'| cut
-d":" -f1
hello2.txt
hello3.txt
```

Matching a Range of Lines

In Chapter 1 you saw how to use the head and tail commands to display a range of lines in a text file. Now suppose that you want to search a range of lines for a string. For instance, the following command displays lines 9 through 15 of longfile.txt:

```
cat -n longfile.txt |head -15|tail -9
```

The output is here:

```
     7    and each line
     8    contains
     9    one or
    10    more words
    11    and if you
    12    use the cat
    13    command the
    14    file contents
    15    scroll
```

This command displays the subset of lines 9 through 15 of longfile.txt that contain the string and:

```
cat -n longfile.txt |head -15|tail -9 | grep and
```

The output is here:

```
  7     and each line
 11     and if you
 13     command the
```

This command includes a whitespace after the word and, thereby excluding the line with the word "command":

```
cat -n longfile.txt |head -15|tail -9 | grep "and "
```

The output is here:

```
  7     and each line
 11     and if you
```

Note that the preceding command excludes lines that end in "and" because they do not have the whitespace after "and" at the end of the line. You could remedy this situation with an "OR" operator including both cases:

```
cat -n longfile.txt |head -15|tail -9 | grep " and\|and "
  7     and each line
 11     and if you
 13     command the
```

However, the preceding allows "command" back into the mix. Hence, if you really want to match a specific word, it's best to use the –w tag, which is smart enough to handle the variations:

```
cat -n longfile.txt |head -15|tail -9 | grep -w "and"
  7     and each line
 11     and if you
```

The use of whitespace is safer if you are looking for something at the beginning or end of a line. This is a common approach when reading contents of log files or other structured text where the first word is often important (a tag like ERROR or Warning, a numeric code or a date). This command displays the lines that start with the word and:

```
cat longfile.txt |head -15|tail -9 | grep "^and "
```

The output is here (without the line number because we are not using "cat -n"):

```
and each line
and if you
```

Recall that the "use the file name(s) in the command, instead of using `cat` to display the file first" style is more efficient:

```
head -15 longfile.txt |tail -9 | grep "^and "
and each line
and if you
```

However, the `head` command does not display the line numbers of a text file, so the "cat first" (`cat -n` adds line numbers) style is used in the earlier examples when you want to see the line numbers, even though this style is less efficient. Basically, you only want to add an extra command to a pipe if it is adding value, otherwise it's better to start with a direct call to the files you are trying to process with the first command in the pipe, assuming the command syntax is capable of reading in filenames.

Using Back References in the `grep` Command

The `grep` command allows you to reference a set of characters that match a regular expression placed inside a pair of parentheses. For `grep` to parse the parentheses correctly, each has to be preceded with the escape character "\."

For example, `grep 'a\(.\)'` uses the "." regular expression to match ab or "a3" but not "3a" or "ba."

The back reference '\n,' where n is a single digit, matches the substring previously matched by the nth parenthesized sub-expression of the regular expression. For example, `grep '\(a\)\1'` matches "aa" and `grep '\(a\)\2'` matches "aaa."

When used with alternation, if the group does not participate in the match, then the back reference makes the whole match fail. For example, `grep 'a\(.\)|b\1'` will not match ba or ab or bb (or anything else really).

If you have more than one regular expression inside a pair of parentheses, they are referenced (from left to right) by \1, \2, . . ., \9:

```
grep -e '\([a-z]\)\([0-9]\)\1' is the same as this command:
grep -e '\([a-z]\)\([0-9]\)\([a-z]\)'
grep -e '\([a-z]\)\([0-9]\)\2' is the same as this command:
grep -e '\([a-z]\)\([0-9]\)\([0-9]\)'
```

The easiest way to think of it is that the number (for example, \2) is a placeholder or variable that saves you from typing the longer regular expression it references. As regular expressions can get extremely complex, this often helps code clarity.

You can match consecutive digits or characters using the pattern \([0-9]\)\1. For example, the following command is a successful match because the string "1223" contains a pair of consecutive identical digits:

```
echo "1223" | grep  -e '\([0-9]\)\1'
```

Similarly, the following command is a successful match because the string "12223" contains three consecutive occurrences of the digit 2:

```
echo "12223" | grep  -e '\([0-9]\)\1\1'
```

You can check for the occurrence of two identical digits separated by any character with this expression:

```
echo "12z23" | grep  -e '\([0-9]\).\1'
```

In an analogous manner, you can test for the occurrence of duplicate letters, as shown here:

```
echo "abbc" | grep  -e '\([a-z]\)\1'
```

The following example matches an IP address, and does not use back references, just the "\d" and "\." Regular expressions to match digits and periods are as follows:

```
echo "192.168.125.103" | grep -e
'\(\d\d\d\)\.\(\d\d\d\)\.\(\d\d\d\)\.\(\d\d\d\)'
```

If you want to allow for fewer than three digits, you can use the expression {1,3}, which matches 1, 2, or 3 digits on the third block. In a situation where any of the four blocks might have fewer than three characters, you must use the following type of syntax in all four blocks:

```
echo "192.168.5.103" | grep -e
'\(\d\d\d\)\.\(\d\d\d\)\.\(\d\)\{1,3\}\.\(\d\d\d\)'
```

You can perform more complex matches using back references. Listing 3.3 displays the contents of columns5.txt, which contains several lines that are palindromes (the same spelling from left-to-right as right-to-left). Note that the third line is an empty line.

LISTING 3.3 columns5.txt

```
one eno
ONE ENO
```

```
ONE TWO OWT ENO
four five
```

The following command finds all lines that are palindromes:

```
grep -w -e '\(.\)\(.\).*\2\1' columns5.txt
```

The output of the preceding command is here:

```
one eno
ONE ENO
ONE TWO OWT ENO
```

The idea is as follows: the first \(.\) matches a set of letters, followed by a second \(.\) that matches a set of letters, followed by any number of intermediate characters. The sequence \2\1 reverses the order of the matching sets of letters specified by the two consecutive occurrences of \(.\).

Finding Empty Lines in Datasets

Recall that the metacharacter "^" refers to the beginning of a line and the metacharacter "$" refers to the end of a line. Thus, an empty line consists of the sequence ^$. You can find the single empty in columns5.txt with this command:

```
grep -n "^$" columns5.txt
```

The output of the preceding grep command is here (use the -n switch to display line numbers, as blank lines will not otherwise show in the output):

```
3:
```

More commonly the goal is to simply strip the empty lines from a file. We can do that just by inverting the prior query (and not showing the line numbers):

```
grep -v "^$" columns5.txt
one eno
ONE ENO
ONE TWO OWT ENO
four five
```

As you can see, the preceding output displays four non-empty lines, and as we saw in the previous `grep` command, line #3 is an empty line.

Using Keys to Search Datasets

Data is often organized around unique values (typically numbers) in order to distinguish otherwise similar things: for example, John Smith the *manager* must not be confused with John Smith the *programmer* in an employee dataset. Hence, each record is assigned a unique number that will be used for all queries related to employees. Moreover, their names are merely data elements of a given record, rather than a means of identifying a record that contains a particular person.

With the preceding points in mind, suppose that you have a text file in which each line contains a single key value. In addition, another text file consists of one or more lines, where each line contains a key value followed by a quantity value.

As an illustration, Listing 3.4 displays the contents of skuvalues.txt and Listing 3.5 displays the contents of skusold.txt. Note that an SKU is a term often used to refer to an individual product configuration, including its packaging, labeling, and so forth.

LISTING 3.4 skuvalues.txt

```
4520
5530
6550
7200
8000
```

LISTING 3.5 skusold.txt

```
4520 12
4520 15
5530 5
5530 12
6550 0
6550 8
7200 50
7200 10
7200 30
8000 25
8000 45
8000 90
```

The Backslash Character and the `grep` Command

The "\" character has a special interpretation when it's followed by the following characters:

"\b" = Match the empty string at the edge of a word.

"\B" = Match the empty string provided it's not at the edge of a word, so: "\brat\b" matches the separate word "rat" but not "crate," and "\Brat\B" matches "crate" but not "furry rat."

"\<" = Match the empty string at the beginning of a word.

"\>" = Match the empty string at the end of a word.

"\w" = Match word constituent, it is a synonym for "[_[:alnum:]]."

"\W" = Match non-word constituent, it is a synonym for "[^_[:alnum:]]."

"\s" = Match whitespace, it is a synonym for "[[:space:]]."

"\S" = Match non-whitespace, it is a synonym for "[^[:space:]]."

Multiple Matches in the `grep` Command

In an earlier example you saw how to use the `-i` option to perform a case insensitive match. However, you can also use the pipe "|" symbol to specify more than one sequence of regular expressions.

For example, the following `grep` expression matches any line that contains "one" as well as any line that contains "ONE TWO":

```
grep "one\|ONE TWO" columns5.txt
```

The output of the preceding `grep` command is here:

```
one eno
ONE TWO OWT ENO
```

Although the preceding `grep` command specifies a pair of character strings, you can specify an arbitrary number of character sequences or regular expressions, as long as you put "\|" between each thing you want to match.

The `grep` Command and the `xargs` Command

The `xargs` command is often used in conjunction with the `find` command in bash. For example, you can search for the files under the current directory (including subdirectories) that have the `sh` suffix and then check which one of those files contains the string `abc`, as shown here:

```
find . -print |grep "sh$" | xargs grep -l abc
```

A more useful combination of the find and xargs commands is shown here:

```
find . -mtime -7 -name "*.sh" -print | xargs grep -l abc
```

The preceding command searches for all the files (including subdirectories) with suffix "sh" that have not been modified in at least seven days, and pipes that list to the xargs command, which displays the files that contain the string abc (case insensitive).

The find command supports many options, which can be combined via AND as well as OR in order to create very complex expressions.

Note that grep -R hello . also performs a search for the string hello in all files, including subdirectories, and follows the "one process" recommendation. On the other hand, the find . -print command searches for all files in all subdirectories, and you can pipe the output to xargs grep hello in order to find the occurrences of the word hello in all files (which involves two processes instead of one process).

You can use the output of the preceding code snippet in order to copy the matching files to another directory, as shown here:

```
cp `find . -print |grep "sh$" | xargs grep -l abc` /tmp
```

Alternatively, you can copy the matching files in the current directory (without matching files in any subdirectories) to another directory with the grep command:

```
cp `grep -l abc *sh` /tmp
```

Yet another approach is to use "back tick" so that you can obtain additional information:

```
for file in `find . -print`
do
    echo "Processing the file: $file"
    # now do something here
done
```

Keep in mind that if you pass too many filenames to the xargs command you will see a "too many files" error message. In this situation, try to insert additional grep commands prior to the xargs command in order to reduce the number of files that are piped into the xargs command.

If you work with NodeJS, you know that the `node_modules` directory contains a large number of files. In most cases, you probably want to exclude the files in that directory when you are searching for a string, and the "-v" option is ideal for this situation. The following command excludes the files in the `node_modules` directory while searching for the names of the HTML files that contain the string src and redirecting the list of file names to the file src_list.txt (and also redirecting error messages to /dev/null):

```
find . -print |grep -v node |xargs grep -il src >src_list.txt
2>/dev/null
```

You can extend the preceding command to search for the HTML files that contain the string src and the string angular with the following command:

```
find . -print |grep -v node |xargs grep -il src |xargs grep -il
angular >angular_list.txt 2>/dev/null
```

You can use the following combination of grep and xargs to find the files that contain both xml and defs:

```
grep -l xml *svg |xargs grep -l def
```

A variation of the preceding command redirects error messages to /dev/null, as shown here:

```
grep -l hello *txt 2>/dev/null | xargs grep -c hello
```

Searching Zip Files for a String

There are at least three ways to search for a string in one or more zip files. As an example, suppose that you want to determine which zip files contain SVG documents.

The first way is shown here:

```
for f in `ls *zip`
do
    echo "Searching $f"
    jar tvf $f |grep "svg$"
done
```

When there are many zip files in a directory, the output of the preceding loop can be very verbose, in which case you need to scroll backward and probably copy/paste the names of the files that actually contain SVG documents into a separate file. A better solution is to put the preceding loop in a shell and redirect its output. For instance, create the file `findsvg.sh` whose contents are the preceding loop, and then invoke this command:

```
./findsvg.sh 1>1 2>2
```

Notice that the preceding command redirects error message (2>) to the file 2 and the results of the jar/grep command (1>) to the file 1. See the Appendix for another example of searching zip files for SVG documents.

Checking for a Unique Key Value

Sometimes you need to check for the existence of a string (such as a key) in a text file, and then perform additional processing based on its existence. However, do not assume that the existence of a string means that that string only occurs once. As a simple example, suppose the file `mykeys.txt` has the following content:

```
2000
22000
10000
3000
```

Suppose that you search for the string 2000, which you can do with `findkey.sh`, whose contents are displayed in Listing 3.6.

LISTING 3.6 findkey.sh

```
key="2000"
if [ "`grep $key mykeys.txt`" != "" ]
then
  foundkey=true
else
    foundkey=false
fi
echo "current key = $key"
echo "found key    = $foundkey"
```

Listing 3.6 contains if/else conditional logic to determine whether or not the file `mykeys.txt` contains the value of `$key` (which is initialized as 2000). Launch the code in Listing 3.6 and you will see the following output:

```
current key = 2000
found key    = true
linecount    = 2
```

While the key value of 2000 does exist in `mykeys.txt`, you can see that it matches two lines in `mykeys.txt`. However, if `mykeys.txt` were part of a file with 100,000 (or more) lines, it's not obvious that the value of 2000 matches more than one line. In this dataset, 2000 and 22000 both match, and you can prevent the extra matching line with this code snippet:

```
grep -w $key
```

Thus, in files that have duplicate lines, you can count the number of lines that match the key via the preceding code snippet. Another way to do so involves the use of `wc -1`, which displays the line count.

Redirecting Error Messages

Another scenario involves the use of the `xargs` command with the `grep` command, which can result in "no such . . ." error messages:

```
find . -print |xargs grep -il abc
```

Make sure to redirect errors using the following variant:

```
find . -print |xargs grep -il abc 2>/dev/null
```

The `egrep` Command and the `fgrep` Command

The `egrep` command is an Extended `grep` that supports added `grep` features like "+" (1 or more occurrence of previous character), "?" (0 or 1 occurrence of previous character), and "|" (alternate matching). The `egrep` command is almost identical to the `grep -E`, along with some caveats that are described here:

> *https://www.gnu.org/software/grep/manual/html_node/Basic-vs-Extended.html.*

One advantage of using the `egrep` command is that it's easier to understand the regular expressions than the corresponding expressions in `grep` (when it's combined with backward references).

The `egrep` ("extended `grep`") command supports extended regular expressions, as well as the pipe "|" in order to specify multiple words in a search pattern. A match is successful if any of the words in the search pattern appear, so you can think of the search pattern as an "any" match. Thus, the pattern "`abc|def`" matches lines that contain either `abc` or `def` (or both).

For example, the following code snippet enables you to search for occurrences of the string `abc` as well as occurrences of the string `def` in all files with the suffix `sh`:

```
egrep -w 'abc|def' *sh
```

The preceding `egrep` command is an "or" operation: a line matches if it contains either abc *or* def.

You can also use metacharacters in `egrep` expressions. For example, the following code snippet matches lines that start with `abc` or end with four and a whitespace:

```
egrep '^123|four $' columns3.txt
```

A more detailed explanation of grep, egrep, and frep is here:

> *https://superuser.com/questions/508881/*
> *what-is-the-difference-between-grep-pgrep-egrep-fgrep.*

Displaying "Pure" Words in a Dataset with `egrep`

For simplicity, let's work with a text string, and that way we can see the intermediate results as we work toward the solution. Let's initialize the variable x as shown here:

```
x="ghi abc Ghi 123 #def5 123z"
```

The first step is to split x into words:

```
echo $x |tr -s ' ' '\n'
```

The output is here:

```
ghi
abc
Ghi
123
#def5
123z
```

The second step is to invoke `egrep` with the regular expression `^[a-zA-Z]+`, which matches any string consisting of one or more uppercase and/or lowercase letters (and nothing else):

```
echo $x |tr -s ' ' '\n' |egrep "^[a-zA-Z]+$"
```

The output is here:

```
ghi
abc
Ghi
```

If you also want to sort the output and print only the unique words, use this command:

```
echo $x |tr -s ' ' '\n' |egrep "^[a-zA-Z]+$" |sort | uniq
```

The output is here:

```
123
123z
Ghi
abc
ghi
```

If you want to extract only the integers in the variable x, use this command:

```
echo $x |tr -s ' ' '\n' |egrep "^[0-9]+$" |sort | uniq
```

The output is here:

```
123
```

If you want to extract alphanumeric words from the variable x, use this command:

```
echo $x |tr -s ' ' '\n' |egrep "^[a-zA-Z0-9]+$" |sort | uniq
```

The output is here:

```
123
123z
Ghi
abc
ghi
```

Note that the ASCII collating sequences place digits before uppercase letters, and the latter are before lowercase letters for the following reason: 0 through 9 are hexadecimal values 0x30 through 0x39, and the uppercase letters in A-Z are hexadecimal 0x41 through 0x5a, and the lowercase letters in a-z are hexadecimal 0x61 through 0x7a.

Now you can replace `echo $x` with a dataset in order to retrieve only alphabetic strings from that dataset.

The `fgrep` Command

The `fgrep` ("fast grep") is the same as `grep -F` and although fgrep is deprecated, it's still supported in order to allow historical applications that rely on them to run unmodified. In addition, some older systems might not support the –F option for the `grep` command, so they use the `fgrep` command. If you really want to learn more about the `fgrep` command, perform an Internet search for tutorials.

A Simple Use Case

The code sample in this section shows you how to use the `grep` command in order to find specific lines in a dataset and then "merge" pairs of lines to create a new dataset. This is very much like what a "join" command does in a relational database. Listing 3.7 displays the contents of the file `test1.csv`, which contains the initial dataset.

LISTING 3.7 *test1.csv*

```
F1,F2,F3,M0,M1,M2,M3,M4,M5,M6,M7,M8,M9,M10,M11,M12
1,KLM,,1.4,,0.8,,1.2,,1.1,,,2.2,,,1.4
1,KLMAB,,0.05,,0.04,,0.05,,0.04,,,0.07,,,0.05
1,TP,,7.4,,7.7,,7.6,,7.6,,,8.0,,,7.3
1,XYZ,,4.03,3.96,,3.99,,3.84,4.12,,,,4.04,,
2,KLM,,0.9,0.7,,0.6,,0.8,0.5,,,,0.5,,
2,KLMAB,,0.04,0.04,,0.03,,0.04,0.03,,,,0.03,,
2,EGFR,,99,99,,99,,99,99,,,,99,,
2,TP,,6.6,6.7,,6.9,,6.6,7.1,,,,7.0,,
3,KLM,,0.9,0.1,,0.5,,0.7,,0.7,,,0.9,,
3,KLMAB,,0.04,0.01,,0.02,,0.03,,0.03,,,0.03,,
3,PLT,,224,248,,228,,251,,273,,,206,,
3,XYZ,,4.36,4.28,,4.58,,4.39,,4.85,,,4.47,,
3,RDW,,13.6,13.7,,13.8,,14.1,,14.0,,,13.4,,
3,WBC,,3.9,6.5,,5.0,,4.7,,3.7,,,3.9,,
3,A1C,,5.5,5.6,,5.7,,5.6,,5.5,,,5.3,,
4,KLM,,1.2,,0.6,,0.8,0.7,,,0.9,,,1.0,
4,TP,,7.6,,7.8,,7.6,7.3,,,7.7,,,7.7,
5,KLM,,0.7,,0.8,,1.0,0.8,,,0.5,,,1.1,,
```

```
5,KLM,,0.03,,0.03,,0.04,0.04,,0.02,,,0.04,,
5,TP,,7.0,,7.4,,7.3,7.6,,7.3,,,7.5,,
5,XYZ,,4.73,,4.48,,4.49,4.40,,,4.59,,,4.63,
```

Listing 3.8 displays the contents of the file `joinlines.sh`, which illustrates how to merge the pairs of matching lines in `joinlines.csv`.

LISTING 3.8 joinlines.sh

```
inputfile="test1.csv"
outputfile="joinedlines.csv"
tmpfile2="tmpfile2"

# patterns to match:
klm1="1,KLM,"
klm5="5,KLM,"
xyz1="1,XYZ,"
xyz5="5,XYZ,"

#output:
#klm1,xyz1
#klm5,xyz5

# step 1: match patterns with CSV file:
klm1line="`grep $klm1 $inputfile`"
klm5line="`grep $klm5 $inputfile`"
xyz1line="`grep $xyz1  $inputfile`"
# $xyz5 matches 2 lines (we want first line):
grep $xyz5 $inputfile > $tmpfile2
xyz5line="`head -1 $tmpfile2`"
echo "klm1line: $klm1line"
echo "klm5line: $klm5line"
echo "xyz1line: $xyz1line"
echo "xyz5line: $xyz5line"

# step 3: create summary file:
echo "$klm1line" | tr -d '\n' > $outputfile
echo "$xyz1line"                >> $outputfile
echo "$klm5line" | tr -d '\n' >> $outputfile
echo "$xyz5line"                >> $outputfile
echo; echo
```

The output from launching the shell script in Listing 3.8 is here:

```
1,KLM,,1.4,,0.8,,1.2,,1.1,,,2.2,,,1.41,
XYZ,,4.03,3.96,,3.99,,3.84,4.12,,,,,4.04,,
5,KLM,,0.7,,0.8,,1.0,0.8,,0.5,,,1.1,,5,KLM,,0.03,,0.03,,0.04,0
.04,,0.02,,,0.04,,5,XYZ,4.73,,4.48,,4.49,4.40,,,4.59,,,4.63,
```

As you can see, the task in this section is very easily solved via the grep command. Note that additional data cleaning is required in order to handle the empty fields in the output.

Summary

This chapter showed you how to work with the grep utility, which is a very powerful Unix command for searching text fields for strings. You saw various options for the grep command, and examples of how to use those options to find string patterns in text files.

Next you learned about egrep, which is a variant of the grep command, which can simplify and also expand on the basic functionality of grep, indicating when you might choose one option over another.

Finally, you learned how to use key values in one text file to search for matching lines of text in another file, and perform join-like operations using the grep command.

CHAPTER 4

TRANSFORMING DATA WITH sed

In the prior chapter, we learned how to reduce a stream of data to only the contents that interested us. In this chapter, we learn how to transform that data using the Unix sed utility, which is an acronym for "stream editor."

The first part of this chapter contains basic examples of the sed command, such as replacing and deleting strings, numbers, and letters. The second part of this chapter discusses various switches that are available for the sed command, along with an example of replacing multiple delimiters with a single delimiter in a dataset.

In the final section you will see a number of examples of how to perform stream-oriented processing on datasets, bringing the capabilities of sed together with the commands and regular expressions from prior chapters to accomplish difficult tasks with relatively simple code.

What Is the sed Command?

The name sed is an acronym for "stream editor," and the utility derives many of its commands from the ed line-editor (ed was the first UNIX text editor). The sed command is a "non-interactive" stream-oriented editor that can be used to automate editing via shell scripts. This ability to modify an entire stream of data (which can be the contents of multiple files, in a manner similar to how grep behaves) as if you were inside an editor is not common in modern programming languages. This behavior allows some capabilities not easily duplicated elsewhere, while behaving exactly like any other command (grep, cat, ls, find, and so forth) in how it can accept data, output data, and pattern match with regular expressions.

Some of the more common uses for sed include: print matching lines, delete matching lines, and find/replace matching strings or regular expressions.

The sed Execution Cycle

Whenever you invoke the sed command, an execution cycle refers to various options that are specified and executed until the end of the file/input is reached. Specifically, an execution cycle performs the following steps:

Reads an entire line from stdin/file.
Removes any trailing newline.
Places the line in its pattern buffer.
Modifies the pattern buffer according to the supplied commands.
Prints the pattern buffer to stdout.

Matching String Patterns Using sed

The sed command requires you to specify a string in order to match the lines in a file. For example, suppose that the file numbers.txt contains the following lines:

```
1
2
123
3
five
4
```

The following sed command prints all the lines that contain the string 3:

```
cat numbers.txt |sed -n "/3/p"
```

Another way to produce the same result:

```
sed -n "/3/p" numbers.txt
```

In both cases the output of the preceding commands is as follows:

```
123
3
```

As we saw earlier with other commands, it is always more efficient to just read in the file using the sed command than to pipe it in with a different command. You can "feed" it data from another command, provided that other command adds value (such as adding line numbers, removing blank lines, or other similar helpful activities).

The −n option suppresses all output, and the p option prints the matching line. If you omit the −n option, then every line is printed, and the p option causes the matching line to be printed again. Hence, you can issue the following command:

```
sed "/3/p" numbers.txt
```

The output (the data to the right of the colon) is as follows. Note that the labels to the left of the colon show the source of the data, to illustrate the "one row at a time" behavior of sed.

```
Basic stream output :1
Basic stream output :2
Basic stream output :123
Pattern Matched text:123
Basic stream output :3
Pattern Matched text:3
Basic stream output :five
Basic stream output :4
```

It is also possible to match two patterns and print everything between the lines that match:

```
sed -n "/123/,/five/p" numbers.txt
```

The output of the preceding command (all lines between 123 and five, inclusive) is here:

```
123
3
five
```

Substituting String Patterns Using sed

The examples in this section illustrate how to use sed to substitute new text for an existing text pattern.

```
x="abc"
echo $x |sed "s/abc/def/"
```

The output of the preceding code snippet is here:

```
def
```

In the prior command you have instructed sed to substitute ("s) the first text pattern (/abc) with the second pattern (/def) and no further instructions (/").

Deleting a text pattern is simply a matter of leaving the second pattern empty:

```
echo "abcdefabc" |sed "s/abc//"
```

The result is here:

```
defabc
```

As you see, this only removes the first occurrence of the pattern. You can remove all the occurrences of the pattern by adding the "global" terminal instruction (/g"):

```
echo "abcdefabc" |sed "s/abc//g"
```

The result of the preceding command is here:

```
def
```

Note that we are operating directly on the main stream with this command, as we are not using the -n tag. You can also suppress the main stream with -n and print the substitution, achieving the same output if you use the terminal p (print) instruction:

```
echo "abcdefabc" |sed -n "s/abc//gp"
def
```

For substitutions, either syntax will do, but that is not always true of other commands.

You can also remove digits instead of letters, by using the numeric metacharacters as your regular expression match pattern (from Chapter 1):

```
ls svcc1234.txt |sed "s/[0-9]//g"
ls svcc1234.txt |sed -n "s/[0-9]//gp"
```

The result of either of the two preceding commands is here:

```
svcc.txt
```

Recall that the file `columns4.txt` contains the following text:

```
123 ONE TWO
456 three four
ONE TWO THREE FOUR
five 123 six
one two three
four five
```

The following `sed` command is instructed to identify the rows between 1 and 3, inclusive (`"1,3`), and delete (`d"`) them from the output:

```
cat columns4.txt  | sed "1,3d"
```

The output is here:

```
five 123 six
one two three
four five
```

The following `sed` command deletes a range of lines, starting from the line that matches `123` and continuing through the file until reaching the line that matches the string `five` (and also deleting all the intermediate lines). The syntax should be familiar from the earlier matching example:

```
sed "/123/,/five/d" columns4.txt
```

The output is here:

```
one two three
four five
```

Replacing Vowels from a String or a File

The following code snippet shows you how simple it is to replace multiple vowels from a string using the `sed` command:

```
echo "hello" | sed "s/[aeio]/u/g"
```

The output from the preceding code snippet is here:

```
Hullu
```

Deleting Multiple Digits and Letters from a String

Suppose that we have a variable x that is defined as follows:

```
x="a123zAB 10x b 20 c 300 d 40w00"
```

Recall that an integer consists of one or more digits, so it matches the regular expression [0-9]+, which matches one or more digits. However, you need to specify the regular expression [0-9]* in order to remove every number from the variable x:

```
echo $x | sed "s/[0-9]//g"
```

The output of the preceding command is here:

```
azAB x b  c  d w
```

The following command removes all lowercase letters from the variable x:

```
echo $x | sed "s/[a-z]*//g"
```

The output of the preceding command is here:

```
123AB 10  20  300  4000
```

The following command removes all lowercase and uppercase letters from the variable x:

```
echo $x | sed "s/[a-z][A-Z]*//g"
```

The output of the preceding command is here:

```
123 10  20  300  4000
```

Search and Replace with sed

The previous section showed you how to delete a range of rows of a text file, based on a start line and end line, using either a numeric range or a pair of strings. As deleting is just substituting an empty result for what you match, it should now be clear that a replace activity involves populating that part of the command with something that achieves your desired outcome. This section contains various examples that illustrate how to get the exact substitution you desire.

The following examples illustrate how to convert lowercase abc to upper-case ABC in sed:

```
echo "abc" |sed "s/abc/ABC/"
```

The output of the preceding command is here (which only works on one case of abc):

```
ABC
echo "abcdefabc" |sed "s/abc/ABC/g"
```

The output of the preceding command is here (/g" means works on every case of abc):

```
ABCdefABC
```

The following sed expression performs three consecutive substitutions, using –e to string them together. It changes exactly one (the first) a to A, one b to B, one c to C:

```
echo "abcde" |sed -e "s/a/A/" -e "s/b/B/" -e "s/c/C/"
```

The output of the preceding command is here:

```
ABCde
```

Obviously, you can use the following sed expression that combines the three substitutions into one substitution:

```
echo "abcde" |sed "s/abc/ABC/"
```

Nevertheless, the –e switch is useful when you need to perform more complex substitutions that cannot be combined into a single substitution.

The "/" character is not the only delimiter that sed supports, which is useful when strings contain the "/" character. For example, you can reverse the order of /aa/bb/cc/ with this command:

```
echo "/aa/bb/cc" |sed -n "s#/aa/bb/cc#/cc/bb/aa/#p"
```

The output of the preceding sed command is here:

```
/cc/bb/aa/
```

The following examples illustrate how to use the "w" terminal command instruction to write the sed output to both standard output and also to a named file upper1 if the match succeeds:

```
echo "abcdefabc" |sed "s/abc/ABC/wupper1"
ABCdefabc
```

If you examine the contents of the text file upper1 you will see that it contains the same string ABCdefabc that is displayed on the screen. This two-stream behavior that we noticed earlier with the print ("p") terminal command is unusual, but sometimes useful. It is more common to simply send the standard output to a file using the ">" syntax, as shown in the following (both syntaxes work for a replace operation), but in that case nothing is written to the terminal screen. The previous syntax allows both at the same time:

```
echo "abcdefabc" | sed "s/abc/ABC/" > upper1
echo "abcdefabc" | sed -n "s/abc/ABC/p" > upper1
```

Listing 4.1 displays the contents of update2.sh that replace the occurrence of the string hello with the string goodbye in the files with the suffix txt in the current directory.

LISTING 4.1 update2.sh

```
for f in `ls *txt`
do
   newfile="${f}_new"
   cat $f | sed -n "s/hello/goodbye/gp" > $newfile
   mv $newfile $f
done
```

Listing 4.1 contains a for loop that iterates over the list of text files with the txt suffix. For each such file, initialize the variable newfile that is created by appending the string _new to the first file (represented by the variable f). Next, replace the occurrences of hello with the string goodbye in each file f, and redirect the output to $newfile. Finally, rename $newfile to $f using the mv command.

If you want to perform the update in matching files in all subdirectories, replace the "for" statement with the following:

```
for f in `find . -print |grep "txt$"`
```

Datasets with Multiple Delimiters

Listing 4.2 displays the contents of the dataset `delim1.txt`, which contains multiple delimiters "|", ":", and "^". Listing 4.3 displays the contents of `delimiter1.sh`, which illustrates how to replace the various delimiters in `delimiter1.txt` with a single comma delimiter ",".

LISTING 4.2 delimiter1.txt

```
1000|Jane:Edwards^Sales
2000|Tom:Smith^Development
3000|Dave:Del Ray^Marketing
```

LISTING 4.3 delimiter1.sh

```
inputfile="delimiter1.txt"
cat $inputfile | sed -e 's/:/,/' -e 's/|/,/' -e 's/\^/,/'
```

As you can see, the second line in Listing 4.3 is simple yet very powerful: you can extend the `sed` command with as many delimiters as you require in order to create a dataset with a single delimiter between values. The output from Listing 4.3 is shown here:

```
1000,Jane,Edwards,Sales
2000,Tom,Smith,Development
3000,Dave,Del Ray,Marketing
```

Do keep in mind that this kind of transformation can be a bit unsafe unless you have checked that your new delimiter is *not* already in use. For that a `grep` command is useful (you want result to be zero):

```
grep -c ',' $inputfile
0
```

Useful Switches in sed

The three command line switches `-n`, `-e`, and `-i` are useful when you specify them with the `sed` command.

As a review, specify `-n` when you want to suppress the printing of the basic stream output:

```
sed -n 's/foo/bar/'
```

Specify -n and end with /p' when you want to match the result only:

```
sed -n 's/foo/bar/p'
```

We briefly touched on using -e to do multiple substitutions, but it can also be used to combine other commands. This syntax lets us separate the commands in the last example:

```
sed -n -e 's/foo/bar/' -e 'p'
```

A more advanced example that hints at the flexibility of sed involves the insertion of a character after a fixed number of positions. For example, consider the following code snippet:

```
echo "ABCDEFGHIJKLMNOPQRSTUVWXYZ" | sed "s/.\{3\}/&\n/g"
```

The output from the preceding command is here:

```
ABCnDEFnGHInJKLnMNOnPQRnSTUnVWXnYZ
```

While the above example does not seem especially useful, consider a large text stream with no line breaks (everything on one line). You could use something like this to insert newline characters, or something else to break the data into easier to process chunks. It is possible to work through exactly what sed is doing by looking at each element of the command and comparing it to the output, even if you don't know the syntax. (Tip: sometimes you will encounter very complex instructions for sed without any documentation in the code: try not to be that person when coding.)

The output is changing after every three characters and we know dot (.) matches any single character, so .{3} must be telling it to do that (with escape slashes \ because brackets are a special character for sed, and it won't interpret it properly if we just leave it as .{3}. The "n" is clear enough in the replacement column, so the "&\" must be somehow telling it to insert a character instead of replacing it. The terminal g command of course means to repeat. To clarify and confirm those guesses, take what you could infer and perform an Internet search.

Working with Datasets

The sed utility is very useful for manipulating the contents of text files. For example, you can print ranges of lines, and subsets of lines that match a regular expression. You can also perform search-and-replace on the lines in a text file. This section contains examples that illustrate how to perform such functionality.

Printing Lines

Listing 4.4 displays the contents of test4.txt (doubled-spaced lines) that are used for several examples in this section.

LISTING 4.4 test4.txt

```
abc

def

abc

abc
```

The following code snippet prints the first 3 lines in test4.txt (we used this syntax before when deleting rows; it is equally useful for printing):

```
cat test4.txt  |sed -n "1,3p"
```

The output of the preceding code snippet is here (the second line is blank):

```
abc

def
```

The following code snippet prints lines 3 through 5 in test4.txt:

```
cat test4.txt  |sed -n "3,5p"
```

The output of the preceding code snippet is here:

```
def

abc
```

The following code snippet takes advantage of the basic output stream and the second match stream to duplicate every line (including blank lines) in test4.txt:

```
cat test4.txt  |sed "p"
```

The output of the preceding code snippet is here:

```
abc
abc

def
def

abc
abc

abc
abc
```

The following code snippet prints the first three lines and then capitalizes the string abc, duplicating ABC in the final output because we did not use -n and did end with /p" in the second sed command. Remember that /p" only prints the text that matched the sed command, where the basic output prints the whole file, which is why def does not get duplicated:

```
cat test4.txt  |sed -n "1,3p" |sed "s/abc/ABC/p"
ABC
ABC

def
```

Character Classes and sed

You can also use regular expressions with sed. As a reminder, here are the contents of columns4.txt:

```
123 ONE TWO
456 three four
ONE TWO THREE FOUR
five 123 six
one two three
four five
```

As our first example involving sed and character classes, the following code snippet illustrates how to match lines that contain lowercase letters:

```
cat columns4.txt | sed -n '/[0-9]/p'
```

The output from the preceding snippet is here:

```
one two three
one two
one two three four
one
```

```
one three
one four
```

The following code snippet illustrates how to match lines that contain lowercase letters:

```
cat columns4.txt | sed -n '/[a-z]/p'
```

The output from the preceding snippet is here:

```
123 ONE TWO
456 three four
five 123 six
```

The following code snippet illustrates how to match lines that contain the numbers 4, 5, or 6:

```
cat columns4.txt | sed -n '/[4-6]/p'
```

The output from the preceding snippet is here:

```
456 three four
```

The following code snippet illustrates how to match lines that start with any two characters followed by EE:

```
cat columns4.txt | sed -n '/^.\{2\}EE*/p'
```

The output from the preceding snippet is here:

```
ONE TWO THREE FOUR
```

Removing Control Characters

Listing 4.5 displays the contents of `controlchars.txt` that we used before in Chapter 2. Control characters of any kind can be removed by sed just like any other character.

LISTING 4.5 controlchars.txt

```
1 carriage return^M
2 carriage return^M
1 tab character^I
```

The following command removes the carriage return and the tab characters from the text file `ControlChars.txt`:

```
cat controlChars.txt | sed "s/^M//" |sed "s/    //"
```

You cannot see the tab character in the second `sed` command in the preceding code snippet; however, if you redirect the output to the file `nocontrol1.txt`, you can see that there are no embedded control characters in this new file by typing the following command:

```
cat -t nocontrol1.txt
```

Counting Words in a Dataset

Listing 4.6 displays the contents of `WordCountInFile.sh`, which illustrates how to combine various `bash` commands in order to count the words (and their occurrences) in a file.

LISTING 4.6 wordcountinfile.sh

```
# The file is fed to the "tr" command, which changes uppercase to
lowercase
# sed removes commas and periods, then changes whitespace to
newlines
# uniq needs each word on its own line to count the words properly
# Uniq converts data to unique words and the number of times they
appeared
# The final sort orders the data by the wordcount.

cat "$1" | xargs -n1 | tr A-Z a-z | \
sed -e 's/\.//g' -e 's/\,//g' -e 's/ /\ /g' | \
sort | uniq -c | sort -nr
```

The previous command performs the following operations:

- List each word in each line of the file,
- shift characters to lowercase,
- filter out periods and commas,
- change space between words to linefeed, and
- remove duplicates, prefix occurrence count, and sort numerically.

Back References in sed

In the chapter describing `grep` you learned about back references, and similar functionality is available with the `sed` command. The main difference is that the back references can also be used in the replacement section of the command.

The following `sed` command matches the consecutive "a" letters and prints four of them:

```
echo "aa" |sed -n "s#\([a-z]\)\1#\1\1\1\1#p"
```

The output of the preceding code snippet is here:
aaaa

The following `sed` command replaces all duplicate pairs of letters with the letters `aa`:

```
echo "aa/bb/cc" |sed -n "s#\(aa\)/\(bb\)/\(cc\)#\1/\1/\1/#p"
```

The output of the previous `sed` command is here (note the trailing "/" character):

```
aa/aa/aa/
```

The following command inserts a comma in a four-digit number:

```
echo "1234" |sed -n "s@\([0-9]\)\([0-9]\)\([0-9]\)\
([0-9]\)@\1,\2\3\4@p"
```

The preceding `sed` command uses the @ character as a delimiter. The character class [0-9] matches one single digit. Since there are four digits in the input string 1234, the character class [0-9] is repeated 4 times, and the value of each digit is stored in \1, \2, \3, and \4. The output from the preceding `sed` command is here:

```
1,234
```

A more general `sed` expression that can insert a comma in five-digit numbers is here:

```
echo "12345" | sed 's/\([0-9]\{3\}\)$/,\1/g;s/^,//'
```

The output of the preceding command is here:

```
12,345
```

Displaying Only "Pure" Words in a Dataset

In the previous chapter we solved this task using the `egrep` command, and this section shows you how to solve this task using the `sed` command.

For simplicity, let's work with a text string, and that way we can see the intermediate results as we work toward the solution. The approach will be similar to the code block shown earlier that counted unique words. Let's initialize the variable x as shown here:

```
x="ghi abc Ghi 123 #def5 123z"
```

The first step is to split x into one word per line by replacing space with newlines:

```
echo $x |tr -s ' ' '\n'
```

The output is here:

```
ghi
abc
Ghi
123
#def5
123z
```

The second step is to invoke old with the regular expression ^[a-zA-Z]+, which matches any string consisting of one or more uppercase and/or lowercase letters (and nothing else). Note that the -E switch is needed to parse this kind of regular expression in sed, as it uses some of the newer/modern regular expression syntax not available when sed was new.

```
echo $x |tr -s ' ' '\n' |sed -nE "s/(^[a-zA-Z]
[a-zA-Z]*$)/\1/p"
```

The output is here:

```
ghi
abc
Ghi
```

If you also want to sort the output and print only the unique words, pipe the result to the sort and uniq commands:

```
echo $x |tr -s ' ' '\n' |sed -nE "s/(^[a-zA-Z]
[a-zA-Z]*$)/\1/p"|sort|uniq
```

The output is here:

```
Ghi
abc
ghi
```

If you want to extract only the integers in the variable x, use this command:

```
echo $x |tr -s ' ' '\n' |sed -nE "s/(^[0-9][0-9]*$)/\1/p"
|sort|uniq
```

The output is here:

```
123
```

If you want to extract alphanumeric words from the variable x, use this command:

```
echo $x |tr -s ' ' '\n' |sed -nE "s/(^[0-9a-zA-Z]
[0-9a-zA-Z]*$)/\1/p"|sort|uniq
```

The output is here:

```
123
123z
Ghi
abc
ghi
```

Now you can replace echo $x with a dataset in order to retrieve only alphabetic strings from that dataset.

One-Line sed Commands

This section is intended to show a lot of the more useful problems you can solve with a single line of sed, and to expose you to yet more switches and arguments that you can mix and match to solve related tasks.

Moreover, sed supports other options (which are beyond the scope of this book) to perform many other tasks, some of which are sophisticated and correspondingly complex. If you encounter something that none of the examples in this chapter cover, but it seems like the sort of thing sed might do, the odds are decent that it does: an Internet search along the lines of "how do I do <xxx> in sed" will likely either point you in the right direction, or at least to an alternative bash command that will be helpful.

Listing 4.7 displays the contents of data4.txt that are referenced in some of the sed commands in this section. Note that some examples contain options that have not been discussed earlier in this chapter: they are included in case you need the desired functionality (and you can find more details by reading online tutorials).

LISTING 4.7 data4.txt

```
hello world4
        hello world5 two
 hello world6 three
                    hello world4 four
line five
line six
line seven
```

Print the first line of `data4.txt` with this command:

```
sed q < data4.txt
```

The output is here:

```
  hello world3
```

Print the first three lines of `data4.txt` with this command:

```
sed 3q < data4.txt
```

The output is here:

```
  hello world4
     hello world5 two
 hello world6 three
```

Print the last line of `data4.txt` with this command:

```
sed '$!d' < data4.txt
```

The output is here:

```
line seven
```

You can also use this snippet to print the last line:

```
sed -n '$p' < data4.txt
```

Print the last two lines of `data4.txt` with this command:

```
sed '$!N;$!D' <data4.txt
```

The output is here:

```
line six
line seven
```

Print the lines of data4.txt that do not contain world with this command:

```
sed '/world/d' < data4.txt
```

The output is here:

```
line five
line six
line seven
```

Print duplicates of the lines in data4.txt that contain the word world with this command:

```
sed '/world/p' < data4.txt
```

The output is here:

```
    hello world4
    hello world4
     hello world5 two
     hello world5 two
 hello world6 three
 hello world6 three
              hello world4 four
              hello world4 four
line five
line six
line seven
```

Print the fifth line of data4.txt with this command:

```
sed -n '5p' < data4.txt
```

The output is here:

```
line five
```

Print the contents of data4.txt and duplicate line five with this command:

```
sed '5p' < data4.txt
```

The output is here:

```
    hello world4
     hello world5 two
 hello world6 three
              hello world4 four
```

```
line five
line five
line six
line seven
```

Print lines four through six of `data4.txt` with this command:

```
sed -n '4,6p' < data4.txt
```

The output is here:

```
        hello world4 four
line five
line six
```

Delete lines four through six of `data4.txt` with this command:

```
sed '4,6d' < data4.txt
```

The output is here:

```
  hello world4
    hello world5 two
 hello world6 three
line seven
```

Delete the section of lines between `world6` and `six` in `data4.txt` with this command:

```
sed '/world6/,/six/d' < data4.txt
```

The output is here:

```
  hello world4
    hello world5 two
line seven
```

Print the section of lines between `world6` and `six` of `data4.txt` with this command:

```
sed -n '/world6/,/six/p' < data4.txt
```

The output is here:

```
hello world6 three
        hello world4 four
line five
line six
```

Print the contents of data4.txt *and* duplicate the section of lines between world6 and six with this command:

```
sed '/world6/,/six/p' < data4.txt
```

The output is here:

```
    hello world4
     hello world5 two
 hello world6 three
 hello world6 three
            hello world4 four
            hello world4 four
line five
line five
line six
line six
line seven
```

Delete the even-numbered lines in data4.txt with this command:

```
sed 'n;d;' <data4.txt
```

The output is here:

```
    hello world4
 hello world6 three
line five
line seven
```

Replace letters a through m with a ", " with this command:

```
sed "s/[a-m]/,/g" <data4.txt
```

The output is here:

```
    ,,,,o wor,,4
     ,,,,o wor,,5 two
 ,,,,o wor,,6 t,r,,
            ,,,,o wor,,4 ,our
,,n, ,,v,
,,n, s,x
,,n, s,v,n
```

Replace letters a through m with the characters ", @#" with this command:

```
sed "s/[a-m]/,@#/g" <data4.txt
```

The output is here:

```
,@#,@#,@#,@#o wor,@#,@#4
  ,@#,@#,@#,@#o wor,@#,@#5 two
 ,@#,@#,@#,@#o wor,@#,@#6 t,@#r,@#,@#
        ,@#,@#,@#,@#o wor,@#,@#4 ,@#our
,@#,@#,@#n,@# ,@#,@#v,@#
,@#,@#,@#n,@# s,@#x
,@#,@#,@#n,@# s,@#v,@#n
```

The sed command does not recognize escape sequences such as \t, which means that you must literally insert a tab on your console. In the case of the bash shell, enter the control character ^V and then press the <TAB> key in order to insert a <TAB> character.

Delete the tab characters in data4.txt with this command:

```
sed 's/  //g' <data4.txt
```

The output is here:

```
  hello world4
hello world5 two
 hello world6 three
hello world4 four
line five
line six
line seven
```

Delete the tab characters and blank spaces in data4.txt with this command:

```
sed 's/ //g' <data4.txt
```

The output is here:

```
helloworld4
helloworld5two
helloworld6three
helloworld4four
linefive
linesix
lineseven
```

Replace every line of data4.txt with the word pasta with this command:

```
sed 's/.*/\pasta/' < data4.txt
```

The output is here:

```
pasta
pasta
pasta
pasta
pasta
pasta
pasta
```

Insert two blank lines after the third line and one blank line after the fifth line in data4.txt with this command:

```
sed '3G;3G;5G' < data4.txt
```

The output is here:

```
    hello world4
      hello world5 two
hello world6 three


          hello world4 four
line five

line six
line seven
```

Insert a blank line after every line of data4.txt with this command:

```
sed G < data4.txt
```

The output is here:

```
    hello world4

      hello world5 two

    hello world6 three

          hello world4 four

line five

line six

line seven
```

Insert a blank line after every other line of data4.txt with this command:

```
sed n\;G < data4.txt
```

The output is here:

```
    hello world4
      hello world5 two
```

```
hello world6 three
        hello world4 four

line five
line six

line seven
```

Reverse the lines in `data4.txt` with this command:

```
sed '1! G; h;$!d' < data4.txt
```

The output of the preceding `sed` command is here:

```
line seven
line six
line five
        hello world4 four
 hello world6 three
    hello world5 two
    hello world4
```

Summary

This chapter introduced you to the `sed` utility, illustrating the basic tasks of data transformation: allowing additions, removal, and mutation of data by matching individual patterns, or matching the position of the rows in a file, or a combination of the two.

Moreover, we showed that `sed` not only uses regular expressions to match data, similar to the `grep` command, but can also use regular expressions to describe how to transform the data. Finally, there was a list of examples showing both the versatility of the `sed` command, and hopefully communicating the sense that it is an even more flexible and powerful utility than we can show in a single chapter.

CHAPTER 5

DOING EVERYTHING ELSE WITH awk

This chapter introduces you to the awk command, which is a highly versatile utility for manipulating data and restructuring datasets. In fact, this utility is so versatile that entire books have been written about the awk utility. Awk is essentially an entire programming language in a single command, which accepts standard input, gives standard output, and uses regular expressions and metacharacters in the same way other Unix commands do. This lets you plug it into other expressions and do almost anything, at the cost of adding complexity to a command string that may already be doing quite a lot already. It is almost always worthwhile to add a comment when using awk; it is so versatile that it won't be clear which of the many features you are using at a glance.

The first part of this chapter provides a very brief introduction of the awk command. You will learn about some built-in variables for awk, and also how to manipulate string variables using awk. Note that some of these string-related examples can also be handled using other bash commands.

The second part of this chapter shows you conditional logic, while loops, and for loops in awk in order to manipulate the rows and columns in datasets. This section also shows you how to delete lines and merge lines in datasets, and also how to print the contents of a file as a single line of text. You will see how to "join" lines and groups of lines in datasets.

The third section contains code samples that involve metacharacters (introduced in Chapter 1) and character sets in awk commands. You will also see how to use conditional logic in awk commands in order to determine whether or not to print a line of text.

The fourth section illustrates how to "split" a text string that contains multiple "." characters as a delimiter, followed by examples of awk to perform numeric calculations (such as addition, subtraction, multiplication, and division) in files containing numeric data. This section also shows you various numeric functions that are available in awk, and also how to print text in a fixed set of columns.

The fifth section explains how to align columns in a dataset and also how to align and merge columns in a dataset. You will see how to delete columns, how to select a subset of columns from a dataset, and how to work with multiline records in datasets. This section contains some one-line awk commands that can be useful for manipulating the contents of datasets.

The final section of this chapter has a pair of use cases involving nested quotes and date formats in structured data sets.

The awk Command

The awk (Aho, Weinberger, and Kernighan) command has a C-like syntax, and you can use this utility to perform very complex operations on numbers and text strings.

As a side comment, there is also the gawk command which is GNU awk, as well as the nawk command which is "new" awk (neither command is discussed in this book). One advantage of nawk is that it allows you to set externally the value of an internal variable.

Built-In Variables That Control awk

The awk command provides variables that you can change from their default values in order to control how awk performs operations. Examples of such variables (and their default values) include: FS (" "), RS ("\n"), OFS (" "), ORS ("\n"), SUBSEP, and IGNORECASE. The variables FS and RS specify the field separator and record separator, whereas the variables OFS and ORS specify the output field separator and the output record separator, respectively.

You can think of the field separators as delimiters/IFS we used in other commands earlier. The record separators behave in a way similar to how sed treats individual lines—for example sed can match or delete a range of lines instead of matching or deleting something that matches a regular expression (and the default awk record separator is the newline character, so by default `awk` and `sed` have similar ability to manipulate and reference lines in a text file).

As a simple example, you can print a blank line after each line of a file by changing the ORS, from the default of one newline to two newlines, as shown here:

```
cat columns.txt | awk 'BEGIN { ORS ="\n\n" } ; { print $0 }'
```

Other built-in variables include FILENAME (the name of the file that `awk` is currently reading), FNR (the current record number in the current file), NF (the number of fields in the current input record), and NR (the number of input records `awk` has processed since the beginning of the program's execution).

Consult the online documentation for additional information regarding these (and other) arguments for the `awk` command.

How Does the awk Command Work?

The `awk` command reads the input files one record at a time (by default, one record is one line). If a record matches a pattern, then an action is performed (otherwise no action is performed). If the search pattern is not given, then `awk` performs the given actions for each record of the input. The default behavior if no action is given is to print all the records that match the given pattern. Finally, empty braces without any action do nothing; that is, they will not perform the default printing operation. Note that each statement in actions should be delimited by semicolons.

In other to make the preceding paragraph more concrete, here are some simple examples involving text strings and the `awk` command (the results are displayed after each code snippet). The -F switch sets the field separator to whatever follows it, in this case a space. Switches will often provide a shortcut to an action that normally needs a command inside a "BEGIN{}" block:

```
x="a b c d e"
echo $x |awk -F" " '{print $1}'
a
echo $x |awk -F" " '{print NF}'
5
echo $x |awk -F" " '{print $0}'
a b c d e
echo $x |awk -F" " '{print $3, $1}'
c a
```

Now let's change the FS (record separator) to an empty string to calculate the length of a string, this time using the BEGIN{} syntax:

```
echo "abc" | awk 'BEGIN { FS = "" } ; { print NF }'
3
```

The following example illustrates several equivalent ways to specify test. txt as the input file for an awk command:

```
awk < test.txt '{ print $1 }'
awk '{ print $1 }' < test.txt
awk '{ print $1 }' test.txt
```

Yet another way is shown here (but as we've discussed earlier, it can be inefficient, so only do it if the cat command is adding value in some way):

```
cat test.txt | awk '{ print $1 }'
```

This simple example of four ways to do the same task should illustrate why commenting awk calls of any complexity is almost always a good idea. The next person to look at your code may not know/remember the syntax you are using.

Aligning Text with the `printf` Command

Since awk is a programming language inside a single command, it also has its own way of producing formatted output via the printf command.

Listing 5.1 displays the contents of columns2.txt and Listing 5.2 displays the contents of the shell script AlignColumns1.sh, which shows you how to align the columns in a text file.

LISTING 5.1 columns2.txt

```
one two
three four
one two three four
five six
one two three
four five
```

LISTING 5.2 Align Columns1.sh

```
awk '
{
    # left-align  $1 on a 10-char column
    # right-align $2 on a 10-char column
    # right-align $3 on a 10-char column
    # right-align $4 on a 10-char column
    printf("%-10s*%10s*%10s*%10s*\n", $1, $2, $3, $4)
```

```
}
' columns2.txt
```

Listing 5.2 contains a `printf()` statement that displays the first four fields of each row in the file `columns2.txt`, where each field is 10 characters wide.

The output from launching the code in Listing 5.2 is here:

```
one         *         two*          *              *
three       *         four*         *              *
one         *         two*          three*         four*
five        *         six*          *              *
one         *         two*          three*         *
four        *         five*         *              *
```

Keep in mind that `printf` is reasonably powerful and as such has its own syntax, which is beyond the scope of this chapter. A search online can find the manual pages and also discussions of "how to do X with printf()."

Conditional Logic and Control Statements

Like other programming languages, `awk` provides support for conditional logic (if/else) and control statements (for/while loops). `awk` is the only way to put conditional logic inside a piped command stream without creating, installing, and adding to the path a custom executable shell script. The following code block shows you how to use if/else logic:

```
echo "" | awk '
BEGIN { x = 10 }
{
  if (x % 2 == 0) }
    print "x is even"
  }
  else }
    print "x is odd"
  }
}
'
```

The preceding code block initializes the variable x with the value 10 and prints "x is even" if x is divisible by 2, otherwise it prints "x is odd".

The while Statement

The following code block illustrates how to use a `while` loop in `awk`:

```
echo "" | awk '
{
```

```
x = 0
while(x < 4) {
  print "x:",x
  x = x + 1
}
}
'
```

The preceding code block generates the following output:

```
x:0
x:1
x:2
x:3
```

The following code block illustrates how to use a do while loop in awk:

```
echo "" | awk '
{
  x = 0

  do {
    print "x:",x
    x = x + 1
  } while(x < 4)
}
'
```

The preceding code block generates the following output:

```
x:0
x:1
x:2
x:3
```

A for loop in awk

Listing 5.3 displays the contents of Loop.sh, which illustrates how to print a list of numbers in a loop. Note that "i++" is another way of writing "i=i+1" in awk (and most c-derived languages).

LISTING 5.3 Loop.sh

```
awk '
BEGIN {}
{
  for(i=0; i<5; i++) {
    printf("%3d", i)
  }
}
```

```
END { print "\n" }
'
```

Listing 5.3 contains a `for` loop that prints numbers on the same line via the `printf()` statement. Notice that a newline is printed only in the END block of the code. The output from Listing 5.3 is here:

```
0 1 2 3 4
```

A for loop with a break Statement

The following code block illustrates how to use a `break` statement in a `for` loop in `awk`:

```
echo "" | awk '
{
   for(x=1; x<4; x++) {
      print "x:",x
      if(x == 2) {
         break;
      }
   }
}
'
```

The preceding code block prints output only until the variable x has the value 2, after which the loop exits (because of the break inside the conditional logic). The following output is displayed:

```
x:1
```

The next and continue Statements

The following code snippet illustrates how to use `next` and `continue` in a `for` loop in `awk`:

```
awk '
{
   /expression1/ { var1 = 5; next }
   /expression2/ { var2 = 7; next }
   /expression3/ { continue }
   // some other code block here
' somefile
```

When the current line matches `expression1`, then `var1` is assigned the value 5 and `awk` reads the next input line: hence, `expression2` and `expression3` will not be tested. If `expression1` does not match and `expression2` *does* match, then `var2` is assigned the value 7 and then awk will read the next input line. If only expression3 results in a positive match, then awk skips the remaining block of code and processes the next input line.

Deleting Alternate Lines in Datasets

Listing 5.4 displays the contents of linepairs.csv and Listing 5.5 displays the contents of deletelines.sh, which illustrates how to print alternating lines from the dataset linepairs.csv that have exactly two columns.

LISTING 5.4 linepairs.csv

```
a,b,c,d
e,f,g,h
1,2,3,4
5,6,7,8
```

LISTING 5.5 deletelines.sh

```
inputfile="linepairs.csv"
outputfile="linepairsdeleted.csv"
awk ' NR%2 {printf "%s", $0; print ""; next}' < $inputfile > $outputfile
```

Listing 5.5 checks if the current record number NR is divisible by 2, in which case it prints the current line and skips the next line in the dataset. The output is redirected to the specified output file, the contents of which are here:

```
a,b,c,d
1,2,3,4
```

A slightly more common task involves merging consecutive lines, which is the topic of the next section.

Merging Lines in Datasets

Listing 5.6 displays the contents of columns.txt and Listing 5.7 displays the contents of ColumnCount1.sh, which illustrates how to print the lines from the text file columns.txt that have exactly two columns.

LISTING 5.6 columns.txt

```
one two three
one two
```

```
one two three four
one
one three
one four
```

LISTING 5.7 ColumnCount1.sh

```
awk '
{
    if( NF == 2 ) { print $0 }
}
' columns.txt
```

Listing 5.7 is straightforward: if the current record number is even, then the current line is printed (i.e., odd-numbered rows are skipped). The output from launching the code in Listing 5.7 is here:

```
one two
one three
one four
```

If you want to display the lines that do *not* contain 2 columns, use the following code snippet:

```
if( NF != 2 ) { print $0 }
```

Printing File Contents as a Single Line

The contents of test4.txt are here (note the blank lines):

```
abc
def
abc
abc
```

The following code snippet illustrates how to print the contents of test4. txt as a single line:

```
awk '{printf("%s", $0)}' test4.txt
```

The output of the preceding code snippet is here. See if you can tell what is happening before reading the explanation in the next paragraph:

```
Abcdefabcabc
```

Explanation: %s here is the record separator syntax for printf, and having the end quote after it means the record separator is the empty field "". Our default record separator for awk is \n (newline); what the printf is doing is stripping out all the newlines. The blank rows will vanish entirely, as all they have is the newline, so the result is that any actual text will be merged together with nothing between them. Had we added a space between the %s and the ending quote, there would be a space between each character block, plus an extra space for each newline.

Notice how the following comment helps the comprehension of the code snippet:

```
# Merging all text into a single line by removing the newlines
awk '{printf("%s", $0)}' test4.txt
```

Joining Groups of Lines in a Text File

Listing 5.8 displays the contents of digits.txt and Listing 5.9 displays the contents of digits.sh, which "joins" three consecutive lines of text in the file digits.txt.

LISTING 5.8 digits.txt

```
1
2
3
4
5
6
7
8
9
```

LISTING 5.9 digits.sh

```
awk -F" " '{
  printf("%d",$0)
  if(NR % 3 == 0) { printf("\n") }
}' digits.txt
```

Listing 5.9 prints three consecutive lines of text on the same line, after which a linefeed is printed. This has the effect of "joining" every three consecutive lines of text. The output from launching digits.sh is here:

```
123
456
789
```

Joining Alternate Lines in a Text File

Listing 5.10 displays the contents of columns2.txt and Listing 5.11 displays the contents of JoinLines.sh, which "joins" two consecutive lines of text in the file columns2.txt.

LISTING 5.10 columns2.txt

```
one two
three four
one two three four
five six
one two three
four five
```

LISTING 5.11 JoinLines.sh

```
awk '
{
    printf("%s",$0)
    if( $1 !~ /one/) { print " " }
}
' columns2.txt
```

The output from launching Listing 5.11 is here:

```
one two three four
one two three four five six
one two three four five
```

Notice that the code in Listing 5.11 depends on the presence of the string "one" as the first field in alternating lines of text—we are merging based on matching a simple pattern, instead of tying it to record combinations.

To merge each pair of lines instead of merging based on matching a pattern, use the modified code in Listing 5.12.

LISTING 5.12 JoinLines2.sh

```
awk '
BEGIN { count = 0 }
{
    printf("%s",$0)
    if( ++count % 2 == 0) { print " " }
} columns2.txt
```

Yet another way to "join" consecutive lines is shown in Listing 5.13, where the input file and output file refer to files that you can populate with data. This is another example of an awk command that might be a puzzle if encountered in a program without a comment. It is doing exactly the same thing as Listing 5.12, but its purpose is less obvious because of the more compact syntax.

LISTING 5.13 JoinLines2.sh

```
inputfile="linepairs.csv"
outputfile="linepairsjoined.csv"
awk ' NR%2 {printf "%s,", $0; next;}1' < $inputfile >
$outputfile
```

Matching with Metacharacters and Character Sets

If we can match a simple pattern, by now you probably expect that you can also match a regular expression, just as we did in grep and sed. Listing 5.14 displays the contents of Patterns1.sh, which uses metacharacters to match the beginning and the end of a line of text in the file columns2. txt.

LISTING 5.14 Patterns1.sh

```
awk '
    /^f/    { print $1 }
    /two $/ { print $1 }
' columns2.txt
```

The output from launching Listing 5.14 is here:

```
one
five
four
```

Listing 5.15 displays the contents of RemoveColumns.txt with lines that contain a different number of columns.

LISTING 5.15 columns3.txt

```
123 one two
456 three four
one two three four
five 123 six
one two three
four five
```

Listing 5.16 displays the contents of `MatchAlpha1.sh`, which matches text lines that start with alphabetic characters as well as lines that contain numeric strings in the second column.

LISTING 5.16 MatchAlpha1.sh

```
awk '
{
   if( $0 ~ /^[0-9]/) { print $0 }
   if( $0 ~ /^[a-z]+ [0-9]/) { print $0 }
}
' columns3.txt
```

The output from Listing 5.16 is here:

```
123 one two
456 three four
five 123 six
```

Printing Lines Using Conditional Logic

Listing 5.17 displays the contents of `products.txt`, which contains three columns of information.

LISTING 5.17 products.txt

```
MobilePhone 400   new
Tablet      300   new
Tablet      300   used
MobilePhone 200   used
MobilePhone 100   used
```

The following code snippet prints the lines of text in `products.txt` whose second column is greater than 300:

```
awk '$2 > 300' products.txt
```

The output of the preceding code snippet is here:

```
MobilePhone 400   new
```

The following code snippet prints the lines of text in `products.txt` whose product is "new":

```
awk '($3 == "new")' products.txt
```

The output of the preceding code snippet is here:

```
MobilePhone 400   new
Tablet      300   new
```

The following code snippet prints the first and third columns of the lines of text in products.txt whose cost equals 300:

```
awk ' $2 == 300 { print $1, $3 }' products.txt
```

The output of the preceding code snippet is here:

```
Tablet new
Tablet used
```

The following code snippet prints the first and third columns of the lines of text in products.txt that start with the string Tablet:

```
awk '/^Tablet/ { print $1, $3 }' products.txt
```

The output of the preceding code snippet is here:

```
Tablet new
Tablet used
```

Splitting Filenames with awk

Listing 5.18 displays the contents of SplitFilename2.sh, which illustrates how to split a filename containing the "." character in order to increment the numeric value of one of the components of the filename. Note that this code only works for a file name with exactly the expected syntax. It is possible to write more complex code to count the number of segments, or alternately to just say "change the field right before the .zip", which would only require that the filename have a format matching the final two sections (<anystructure>.number.zip).

LISTING 5.18 SplitFilename2.sh

```
echo "05.20.144q.az.1.zip" | awk -F"." '
{
  f5=$5 + 1
  printf("%s.%s.%s.%s.%s.%s",$1,$2,$3,$4,f5,$6)
} '
```

The output from Listing 5.18 is here:

```
05.20.144q.az.2.zip
```

Working with Postfix Arithmetic Operators

Listing 5.19 displays the contents of mixednumbers.txt that contain postfix operators, which means numbers where the negative (and/or positive) sign appears at the end of a column value instead of at the beginning of the number.

LISTING 5.19 mixednumbers.txt

```
324.000-|10|983.000-
453.000-|30|298.000-
783.000-|20|347.000-
```

Listing 5.20 displays the contents of AddSubtract1.sh, which illustrates how to add the rows of numbers in Listing 5.19.

LISTING 5.20 AddSubtract1.sh

```
myFile="mixednumbers.txt"
awk -F"|" '
BEGIN { line = 0; total = 0 }
{
    split($1, arr, "-")
    f1 = arr[1]
    if($1 ~ /-/) { f1 = -f1 }
    line += f1

    split($2, arr, "-")
    f2 = arr[1]
    if($2 ~ /-/) { f2 = -f2 }
    line += f2

    split($3, arr, "-")
    f3 = arr[1]
    if($3 ~ /-/) { f3 = -f3 }
    line += f3

    printf("f1: %d f2: %d f3: %d line: %d\n",f1,f2,f3, line)
    total += line
    line = 0
}
END { print "Total: ",total }
' $myfile
```

The output from Listing 5.20 is here. See if you can work out what the code is doing before reading the explanation that follows:

```
f1: -324 f2: 10 f3: -983 line: -1297
f1: -453 f2: 30 f3: -298 line: -721
f1: -783 f2: 20 f3: -347 line: -1110
Total:  -3128
```

The code assumes we know the format of the file. For each field in a given record, the `split` function returns a vector of length two, where the first position = number, the second position either an empty value or a dash, after which the first position number is "captured" into a variable. The `if` statement just sees if the original field has a dash in it. If the field has a dash, then the numeric variable is made negative, otherwise it is left alone. Then it adds the line up.

Numeric Functions in awk

The `int(x)` function returns the integer portion of a number. If the number is not already an integer, it falls between two integers. Of the two possible integers, the function will return the one closest to zero. This is different from a rounding function, which chooses the closer integer.

For example, `int(3)` is 3, `int(3.9)` is 3, int(-3.9) is -3, and `int(-3)` is -3 as well. An example of the `int(x)` function in an awk command is here:

```
awk 'BEGIN {
    print int(3.534);
    print int(4);
    print int(-5.223);
    print int(-5);
}'
```

The output is here:

```
3
4
-5
-5
```

The `exp(x)` function gives you the exponential of x, or reports an error if x is out of range. The range of values x can have depends on your machine's floating point representation.

```
awk 'BEGIN{
    print exp(123434346);
    print exp(0);
    print exp(-12);
}'
```

The output is here:

```
inf
1
6.14421e-06
```

The `log(x)` function gives you the natural logarithm of x, if x is positive; otherwise, it reports an error (`inf` means infinity and `nan` in output means "not a number").

```
awk 'BEGIN{
    print log(12);
    print log(0);
    print log(1);
    print log(-1);
}'
```

The output is here:

```
2.48491
-inf
0
nan
```

The `sin(x)` function gives you the sine of x and `cos(x)` gives you the cosine of x, with x in radians:

```
awk 'BEGIN {
    print cos(90);
    print cos(45);
}'
```

The output is here:

```
-0.448074
0.525322
```

The `rand()` function gives you a random number. The values of `rand()` are uniformly distributed between 0 and 1: the value is never 0 and never 1.

Often you want random integers instead. Here is a user-defined function you can use to obtain a random, nonnegative integer less than n:

```
function randint(n) {
    return int(n * rand())
}
```

The product produces a random real number greater than 0 and less than n. We then make it an integer (using int) between 0 and n - 1.

Here is an example where a similar function is used to produce random integers between 1 and n:

```
awk '
# Function to roll a simulated die.
```

```
function roll(n) { return 1 + int(rand() * n) }
# Roll 3 six-sided dice and print total number of points.
{
        printf("%d points\n", roll(6)+roll(6)+roll(6))
}'
```

Note that `rand` starts generating numbers from the same point (or "seed") each time `awk` is invoked. Hence, a program will produce the same results each time it is launched. If you want a program to do different things each time it is used, you must change the seed to a value that will be different in each run.

Use the `srand(x)` function to set the starting point, or seed, for generating random numbers to the value x. Each seed value leads to a particular sequence of "random" numbers. Thus, if you set the seed to the same value a second time, you will get the same sequence of "random" numbers again. If you omit the argument x, as in `srand()`, then the current date and time of day are used for a seed. This is how to obtain random numbers that are truly unpredictable. The return value of `srand()` is the previous seed. This makes it easy to keep track of the seeds for use in consistently reproducing sequences of random numbers.

The `time()` function (not in all versions of `awk`) returns the current time in seconds since January 1, 1970. The function `ctime` (not in all versions of `awk`) takes a numeric argument in seconds and returns a string representing the corresponding date, suitable for printing or further processing.

The `sqrt(x)` function gives you the positive square root of x. It reports an error if x is negative. Thus, `sqrt(4)` is 2.

```
awk 'BEGIN{
    print sqrt(16);
    print sqrt(0);
    print sqrt(-12);
}'
```

The output is here:

```
4
0
nan
```

One-Line awk Commands

The code snippets in this section reference the text file `short1.txt`, which you can populate with any data of your choice.

The following code snippet prints each line preceded by the number of fields in each line:

```
awk '{print NF ":" $0}' short1.txt
```

Print the right-most field in each line:

```
awk '{print $NF}' short1.txt
```

Print the lines that contain more than 2 fields:

```
awk '{if(NF > 2) print }' short1.txt
```

Print the value of the right-most field if the current line contains more than 2 fields:

```
awk '{if(NF > 2) print $NF }' short1.txt
```

Remove leading and trailing whitespaces:

```
echo " a b c " | awk '{gsub(/^[ \t]+|[ \t]+$/,"");print}'
```

Print the first and third fields in reverse order for the lines that contain at least 3 fields:

```
awk '{if(NF > 2) print $3, $1}' short1.txt
```

Print the lines that contain the string one:

```
awk '{if(/one/) print }' *txt
```

As you can see from the preceding code snippets, it's easy to extract information or subsets of rows and columns from text files using simple conditional logic and built-in variables in the awk command.

Useful Short awk Scripts

This section contains a set of short awk -based scripts for performing various operations. Some of these scripts can also be used in other shell scripts to perform more complex operations. Listing 5.21 displays the contents of the file data.txt, which is used in various code samples in this section.

LISTING 5.21 data.txt

```
this is line one that contains more than 40 characters
this is line two
this is line three that also contains more than 40 characters
four
```

```
this is line six and the preceding line is empty
line eight and the preceding line is also empty
```

The following code snippet prints every line that is longer than 40 characters:

```
awk 'length($0) > 40' data.txt
```

Now print the length of the longest line in data.txt:

```
awk '{ if (x < length()) x = length() }
END { print "maximum line length is " x }' < data.txt
```

The input is processed by the expand utility to change tabs into spaces, so the widths compared are actually the right-margin columns.

Print every line that has at least one field:

```
awk 'NF > 0' data.txt
```

The preceding code snippet illustrates an easy way to delete blank lines from a file (or rather, to create a new file similar to the old file but from which the blank lines have been removed).

Print seven random numbers from 0 to 100, inclusive:

```
awk 'BEGIN { for (i = 1; i <= 7; i++)
print int(101 * rand()) }'
```

Count the lines in a file:

```
awk 'END { print NR }' < data.txt
```

Print the even-numbered lines in the data file:

```
awk 'NR % 2 == 0' data.txt
```

If you use the expression 'NR % 2 == 1' in the previous code snippet, the program would print the odd-numbered lines.

Insert a duplicate of every line in a text file:

```
awk '{print $0, '\n', $0}' < data.txt
```

Insert a duplicate of every line in a text file and also remove blank lines:

```
awk '{print $0, "\n", $0}' < data.txt | awk 'NF > 0'
```

Insert a blank line after every line in a text file:

```
awk '{print $0, "\n"}' < data.txt
```

Printing the Words in a Text String in `awk`

Listing 5.22 displays the contents of `Fields2.sh`, which illustrates how to print the words in a text string using the `awk` command.

LISTING 5.22 Fields2.sh

```
echo "a b c d e"| awk '
{
  for(i=1; i<=NF; i++) {
     print "Field ",i,":",$i
  }
}
'
```

The output from Listing 5.22 is here:

```
Field  1 : a
Field  2 : b
Field  3 : c
Field  4 : d
Field  5 : e
```

Count Occurrences of a String in Specific Rows

Listing 5.23 and Listing 5.24 display the contents `data1.csv` and `data2.csv`, respectively, and Listing 5.25 displays the contents of `checkrows.sh`, which illustrates how to count the number of occurrences of the string "past" in column 3 in rows 2, 5, and 7.

LISTING 5.23 data1.csv

```
in,the,past,or,the,present
for,the,past,or,the,present
in,the,past,or,the,present
for,the,paste,or,the,future
in,the,past,or,the,present
completely,unrelated,line1
in,the,past,or,the,present
completely,unrelated,line2
```

LISTING 5.24 data2.csv

```
in,the,past,or,the,present
completely,unrelated,line1
for,the,past,or,the,present
completely,unrelated,line2
for,the,paste,or,the,future
in,the,past,or,the,present
```

```
in,the,past,or,the,present
completely,unrelated,line3
```

LISTING 5.25 checkrows.sh

```
files="`ls data*.csv| tr '\n' ' '`"
echo "List of files: $files"
awk -F"," '
( FNR==2 || FNR==5 || FNR==7 ) {
    if ( $3 ~ "past" ) { count++ }
}
END {
    printf "past: matched %d times (INEXACT) ", count
    printf "in field 3 in lines 2/5/7\n"
}' data*.csv
```

Listing 5.25 looks for occurrences in the string past in columns 2, 5, and 7 because of the following code snippet:

```
( FNR==2 || FNR==5 || FNR==7 ) {
    if ( $3 ~ "past" ) { count++ }
}
```

If a match occurs, then the value of count is incremented. The END block reports the number of times that the string past was found in columns 2, 5, and 7. Note that strings such as paste and pasted will match the string past. The output from Listing 5.25 is here:

```
List of files: data1.csv data2.csv
past: matched 5 times (INEXACT) in field 3 in lines 2/5/7
```

The shell script checkrows2.sh replaces the term $3 ~ "past" with the term $3 == "past" in checkrows.sh in order to check for exact matches, which produces the following output:

```
List of files: data1.csv data2.csv
past: matched 4 times (EXACT) in field 3 in lines 2/5/7
```

Printing a String in a Fixed Number of Columns

Listing 5.26 displays the contents of FixedFieldCount1.sh, which illustrates how to print the words in a text string using the awk command.

LISTING 5.26 FixedFieldCount1.sh

```
echo "aa bb cc dd ee ff gg hh"| awk '
BEGIN { colCount = 3 }
{
  for(i=1; i<=NF; i++) {
```

```
    printf("%s ", $i)
    if(i % colCount == 0) {
        print " "
    }
}
}
```

The output from Listing 5.26 is here:

```
aa bb cc
dd ee ff
gg hh
```

Printing a Dataset in a Fixed Number of Columns

Listing 5.27 displays the contents of VariableColumns.txt with lines of text that contain a different number of columns.

LISTING 5.27 VariableColumns.txt

```
this is line one
this is line number one
this is the third and final line
```

Listing 5.28 displays the contents of Fields3.sh, which illustrates how to print the words in a text string using the awk command.

LISTING 5.28 Fields3.sh

```
awk '{printf("%s ", $0)}' | awk '
BEGIN { columnCount = 3 }
{
  for(i=1; i<=NF; i++) {
    printf("%s ", $i)
    if( i % columnCount == 0 )
      print " "
  }
}
' VariableColumns.txt
```

The output from Listing 5.28 is here:

```
this is line
one this is
line number one
this is the
third and final
line
```

Aligning Columns in Datasets

If you have read the preceding two examples, the code sample in this section is easy to understand: you will see how to realign columns of data that are correct in terms of their content, but have been placed in different rows (and therefore are misaligned). Listing 5.29 displays the contents of `mixed-data.csv` with misaligned data values. In addition, the first line and final line in Listing 5.28 are empty lines, which will be removed by the shell script in this section.

LISTING 5.29 mixed-data.csv

```
Sara, Jones, 1000, CA, Sally, Smith, 2000, IL,
Dave, Jones, 3000, FL, John, Jones,
4000, CA,
Dave, Jones, 5000, NY, Mike,
Jones, 6000, NY, Tony, Jones, 7000, WA
```

Listing 5.30 displays the contents of `mixed-data.sh`, which illustrates how to realign the dataset in Listing 5.29.

LISTING 5.30 mixed-data.sh

```
#-------------------------------------------
# 1) remove blank lines
# 2) remove line feeds
# 3) print a LF after every fourth field
# 4) remove trailing ',' from each row
#-------------------------------------------
inputfile="mixed-data.csv"

grep -v "^$" $inputfile |awk -F"," '{printf("%s",$0)}' | awk '
BEGIN { columnCount = 4 }
{
    for(i=1; i<=NF; i++) {
      printf("%s ", $i)
      if( i % columnCount  == 0) { print "" }
    }
}' > temp-columns
# 4) remove trailing ',' from output:
cat temp-columns | sed 's/, $//' | sed 's/ $//' > $outputfile
```

Listing 5.30 starts with a `grep` command that removes blank lines, followed by an `awk` command that prints the rows of the dataset as a single line of text. The second `awk` command initializes the `columnCount` variable with the value 4 in the `BEGIN` block, followed by a `for` loop that iterates through the input fields. After four fields are printed on the same output line, a linefeed is printed, which has the effect of realigning the input dataset as an output dataset consisting of rows that have four fields. The output from Listing 5.30 is here:

```
Sara, Jones, 1000, CA
Sally, Smith, 2000, IL
Dave, Jones, 3000, FL
John, Jones, 4000, CA
Dave, Jones, 5000, NY
Mike, Jones, 6000, NY
Tony, Jones, 7000, WA
```

Aligning Columns and Multiple Rows in Datasets

The preceding section showed you how to realign a dataset so that each row contains the same number of columns and also represents a single data record. The code sample in this section illustrates how to realign columns of data that are correct in terms of their content, and also place two records in each line of the new dataset. Listing 5.31 displays the contents of mixed-data2.csv with misaligned data values, followed by Listing 5.32 that displays the contents of aligned-data2.csv with the correctly formatted dataset.

LISTING 5.31 mixed-data2.csv

```
Sara, Jones, 1000, CA, Sally, Smith, 2000, IL,
Dave, Jones, 3000, FL, John, Jones,
4000, CA,
Dave, Jones, 5000, NY, Mike,
Jones, 6000, NY, Tony, Jones, 7000, WA
```

LISTING 5.32 aligned-data2.csv

```
Sara, Jones, 1000, CA, Sally, Smith, 2000, IL
Dave, Jones, 3000, FL, John, Jones, 4000, CA
Dave, Jones, 5000, NY, Mike, Jones, 6000, NY
Tony, Jones, 7000, WA
```

Listing 5.33 displays the contents of mixed-data2.sh, which illustrates how to realign the dataset in Listing 5.31.

LISTING 5.33 mixed-data2.sh

```
#-------------------------------------------
# 1) remove blank lines
# 2) remove line feeds
# 3) print a LF after every 8 fields
```

```
# 4) remove trailing ',' from each row
#----------------------------------------
inputfile="mixed-data2.txt"
outputfile="aligned-data2.txt"
grep -v "^$" $inputfile |awk -F"," '{printf("%s",$0)}' | awk '
BEGIN { columnCount = 4; rowCount = 2; currRow = 0 }
{
   for(i=1; i<=NF; i++) {
     printf("%s ", $i)
     if( i % columnCount == 0) { ++currRow }
     if(currRow > 0 && currRow % rowCount == 0) {currRow = 0;
print ""}
   }
}' > temp-columns
# 4) remove trailing ',' from output:
cat temp-columns | sed 's/, $//' | sed 's/ $//' > $outputfile
```

Listing 5.33 is very similar to Listing 5.30. The key idea is to print a linefeed character after a pair of "normal" records have been processed, which is implemented via the code that is shown in bold in Listing 5.33.

Now you can generalize Listing 5.33 very easily by changing the initial value of the rowCount variable to any other positive integer, and the code will work correctly without any further modification. For example, if you initialize rowCount to the value 5, then every row in the new dataset (with the possible exception of the final output row) will contain 5 "normal" data records.

Removing a Column from a Text File

Listing 5.34 displays the contents of VariableColumns.txt with lines of text that contain a different number of columns.

LISTING 5.34 VariableColumns.txt

```
this is line one
this is line number one
this is the third and final line
```

Listing 5.35 displays the contents of RemoveColumn.sh that removes the first column from a text file.

LISTING 5.35 RemoveColumn.sh

```
awk '{ for (i=2; i<=NF; i++) printf "%s ", $i; printf "\n"; }'
products.txt
```

The loop is between 2 and NF, which iterates over all the fields except for the first field. In addition, printf explicitly adds newlines. The output of the preceding code snippet is here:

```
400 new
300 new
300 used
200 used
100 used
```

Subsets of Columns of Even Rows in Datasets

Listing 5.35 showed you how to align the rows of a dataset, and the code sample in this section illustrates how to extract a subset of the existing columns and a subset of the rows. Listing 5.36 displays the contents of sub-rows-cols.txt of the desired dataset that contains two columns from every even row of the file aligned-data.txt.

LISTING 5.36 sub-rows-cols.txt

```
Sara, 1000
Dave, 3000
Dave, 5000
Tony, 7000
```

Listing 5.37 displays the contents of sub-rows-cols.sh, which illustrates how to generate the dataset in Listing 5.36. Most of the code is the same as Listing 5.33, with the new code shown in bold.

LISTING 5.37 sub-rows-cols.sh

```
#-----------------------------------------
# 1) remove blank lines
# 2) remove line feeds
# 3) print a LF after every fourth field
# 4) remove trailing ',' from each row
#-----------------------------------------
inputfile="mixed-data.txt"
grep -v "^$" $inputfile |awk -F"," '{printf("%s",$0)}' | awk '
BEGIN { columnCount = 4 }
{
   for(i=1; i<=NF; i++) {
     printf("%s ", $i)
     if( i % columnCount  == 0) { print "" }
   }
}' > temp-columns
# 4) remove trailing ',' from output:
cat temp-columns | sed 's/, $//' | sed 's/$//' > temp-columns2
```

```
cat temp-columns2 | awk '
    BEGIN { rowCount = 2; currRow = 0 }
    {
        if(currRow % rowCount == 0) { print $1, $3 }
        ++currRow
    }' > temp-columns3
    cat temp-columns3 | sed 's/,$//' | sed 's/ $//' >
$outputfile
```

Listing 5.37 contains a new block of code that redirects the output of step #4 to a temporary file `temp-columns2` whose contents are processed by another `awk` command in the last section of Listing 5.37. Notice that the `awk` command contains a `BEGIN` block that initializes the variables `row-Count` and `currRow` with the values 2 and 0, respectively.

The main block prints columns 1 and 3 of the current line if the current row number is even, and then the value of `currRow` is incremented. The output of this `awk` command is redirected to yet another temporary file that is the input to the final code snippet, which uses the `cat` command and two occurrences of the `sed` command in order to remove a trailing ",", and a trailing space, as shown here:

```
cat temp-columns3 | sed 's/,$//' | sed 's/ $//' > $outputfile
```

Keep in mind that there are other ways to perform the functionality in Listing 5.37, and the main purpose is to show you different techniques for combining various bash commands.

Counting Word Frequency in Datasets

Listing 5.38 displays the contents of `WordCounts1.sh`, which illustrates how to count the frequency of words in a file.

LISTING 5.38 WordCounts1.sh

```
awk '
# Print list of word frequencies
{
    for (i = 1; i <= NF; i++)
        freq[$i]++
}
END {
    for (word in freq)
        printf "%s\t%d\n", word, freq[word]
}
' columns2.txt
```

Listing 5.38 contains a block of code that processes the lines in col-umns2.txt. Each time that a word (of a line) is encountered, the code increments the number of occurrences of that word in the hash table `freq`. The END block contains a `for` loop that displays the number of occurrences of each word in `columns2.txt`.

The output from Listing 5.38 is here:

```
two     3
one     3
three   3
six     1
four    3
five    2
```

Listing 5.39 displays the contents of `WordCounts2.sh`, which performs a case insensitive word count.

LISTING 5.39 WordCounts2.sh

```
awk '
{
    # convert everything to lower case
    $0 = tolower($0)
    # remove punctuation
    #gsub(/[^[:alnum:]_[:blank:]]/, "", $0)
    for(i=1; i<=NF; i++) {
        freq[$i]++
    }
}
END {
    for(word in freq) {
        printf "%s\t%d\n", word, freq[word]
    }
}
' columns4.txt
```

Listing 5.39 is almost identical to Listing 5.38, with the addition of the following code snippet that converts the text in each input line to lowercase letters, as shown here:

```
$0 = tolower($0)
```

Listing 5.40 displays the contents of `columns4.txt`.

LISTING 5.40 columns4.txt

```
123 ONE TWO
456 three four
ONE TWO THREE FOUR
five 123 six
```

```
one two three
four five
```

The output from launching Listing 5.39 with `columns4.txt` is here:

```
456    1
two    3
one    3
three  3
six    1
123    2
four   3
five   2
```

Displaying Only "Pure" Words in a Dataset

For simplicity, let's work with a text string and that way we can see the intermediate results as we work toward the solution. This example will be familiar from prior chapters, but now we see how `awk` does it.

Listing 5.41 displays the contents of `onlywords.sh`, which contains three `awk` commands for displaying the words, integers, and alphanumeric strings, respectively, in a text string.

LISTING 5.41 onlywords.sh

```
x="ghi abc Ghi 123 #def5 123z"
echo "Only words:"
echo $x |tr -s ' ' '\n' | awk -F" " '
{
  if($0 ~ /^[a-zA-Z]+$/) { print $0 }
}
' | sort | uniq
echo
echo "Only integers:"
echo $x |tr -s ' ' '\n' | awk -F" " '
{
  if($0 ~ /^[0-9]+$/) { print $0 }
}
' | sort | uniq
echo
echo "Only alphanumeric words:"
echo $x |tr -s ' ' '\n' | awk -F" " '
{
  if($0 ~ /^[0-9a-zA-Z]+$/) { print $0 }
}
' | sort | uniq
echo
```

Listing 5.41 starts by initializing the variable x:

```
x="ghi abc Ghi 123 #def5 123z"
```

The next step is to split x into words:

```
echo $x |tr -s ' ' '\n'
```

The output is here:

```
ghi
abc
Ghi
123
#def5
123z
```

The third step is to invoke `awk` and check for words that match the regular expression `^[a-zA-Z]+`, which matches any string consisting of one or more uppercase and/or lowercase letters (and nothing else):

```
if($0 ~ /^[a-zA-Z]+$/) { print $0 }
```

The output is here:

```
ghi
abc
Ghi
```

Finally, if you also want to sort the output and print only the unique words, redirect the output from the `awk` command to the `sort` command and the `uniq` command.

The second `awk` command uses the regular expression `^[0-9]+` to check for integers and the third `awk` command uses the regular expression `^[0-9a-zA-Z]+` to check for alphanumeric words. The output from launching Listing 5.37 is here:

```
Only words:
Ghi
abc
ghi

Only integers:
123

Only alphanumeric words:
123
```

```
123z
Ghi
abc
ghi
```

Now you can replace the variable x with a dataset in order to retrieve only alphabetic strings from that dataset.

Working with Multiline Records in awk

Listing 5.42 displays the contents of employee.txt and Listing 5.43 displays the contents of Employees.sh, which illustrates how to concatenate text lines in a file.

LISTING 5.42 employees.txt

```
Name:   Jane Edwards
EmpId: 12345
Address: 123 Main Street Chicago Illinois
Name:   John Smith
EmpId: 23456
Address: 432 Lombard Avenue SF California
```

LISTING 5.43 employees.sh

```
inputfile="employees.txt"
outputfile="employees2.txt"
awk '
{
   if($0 ~ /^Name:/) {
     x = substr($0,8) ","
     next
   }
   if( $0 ~ /^Empid:/) {
   #skip the Empid data row
   #x = x substr($0,7)","
     next
   }
   if($0 ~ /^Address:/) {
     x = x substr($0,9)
     print x
   }
}
' < $inputfile > $outputfile
```

The output from launching the code in Listing 5.43 is here:

```
Jane Edwards, 123 Main Street Chicago Illinois
John Smith, 432 Lombard Avenue SF California
```

Now that you have seen a plethora of `awk` code snippets and shell scripts containing the `awk` command that illustrate various types of tasks that you can perform on files and datasets, you are ready for some uses cases. The next section (which is the first use case) shows you how to replace multiple field delimiters with a single delimiter, and the second use case shows you how to manipulate date strings.

A Simple Use Case

The code sample in this section shows you how to use the `awk` command in order to split the comma-separated fields in the rows of a dataset, where fields can contain nested quotes of arbitrary depth.

Listing 5.44 displays the contents of the file `quotes3.csv`, which contains a "," delimiter and multiple quoted fields.

LISTING 5.44 quotes3.csv

```
field5,field4,field3,"field2,foo,bar",field1,field6,field7,"fieldZ"
fname1,"fname2,other,stuff",fname3,"fname4,foo,bar",fname5
"lname1,a,b","lname2,c,d","lname3,e,f","lname4,foo,bar",lname5
```

Listing 5.45 displays the contents of the file `delim1.sh`, which illustrates how to replace the delimiters in `delim1.csv` with a "," character.

LISTING 5.45 delim1.sh

```
#inputfile="quotes1.csv"
#inputfile="quotes2.csv"
inputfile="quotes3.csv"
grep -v "^$" $inputfile |  awk '
{
   print "LINE #" NR ": " $0
   printf ("------------------------\n")
   for (i = 0; ++i <= NF;)
     printf "field #%d : %s\n", i, $i
   printf ("\n")
}' FPAT='([^,]+)|("[^"]+")' < $inputfile
```

The output from launching the shell script in Listing 5.44 is here:

```
LINE #1:
field5,field4,field3,"field2,foo,bar",field1,field6,field7,"fieldZ"
------------------------
field #1 : field5
field #2 : field4
field #3 : field3
field #4 : "field2,foo,bar"
```

```
field #5 : field1
field #6 : field6
field #7 : field7
field #8 : "fieldZ"
LINE #2: fname1,"fname2,other,stuff",fname3,"fname4,foo,bar",
fname5
------------------------------
field #1 : fname1
field #2 : "fname2,other,stuff"
field #3 : fname3
field #4 : "fname4,foo,bar"
field #5 : fname5
LINE #3: "lname1,a,b","lname2,c,d","lname3,e,f","lname4,foo,
bar",lname5
------------------------------
field #1 : "lname1,a,b"
field #2 : "lname2,c,d"
field #3 : "lname3,e,f"
field #4 : "lname4,foo,bar"
field #5 : lname5
LINE #4: "Outer1 "Inner "Inner "Inner C" B" A"
Outer1","XYZ1,c,d","XYZ21name3,e,f"
------------------------------
field #1 : "Outer1 "Inner "Inner "Inner C" B" A" Outer1"
field #2 : "XYZ1,c,d"
field #3 : "XYZ21name3,e,f"
LINE #5:
------------------------------
```

As you can see, the task in this section is very easily solved via the awk command.

Another Use Case

The code sample in this section shows you how to use the awk command in order to reformat the date field in a dataset and change the order of the fields in the new dataset. For example, given the following input line in the original dataset:

```
Jane,Smith,20140805234658
```

The reformatted line in the output dataset has this format:

```
2014-08-05 23:46:58,Jane,Smith
```

Listing 5.46 displays the contents of the file dates2.csv, which contains a "," delimiter and three fields.

LISTING 5.46 dates2.csv

```
Jane,Smith,20140805234658
Jack,Jones,20170805234652
Dave,Stone,20160805234655
John,Smith,20130805234646
Jean,Davis,20140805234649
Thad,Smith,20150805234637
Jack,Pruit,20160805234638
```

Listing 5.47 displays the contents of `string2date2.sh`, which converts the date field to a new format and shifts the new date to the first field.

LISTING 5.47 string2date2.sh

```
inputfile="dates2.csv"
outputfile="formatteddates2.csv"
rm -f $outputfile; touch $outputfile
for line in `cat $inputfile`
do
    fname=`echo $line |cut -d"," -f1`
    lname=`echo $line |cut -d"," -f2`
    date1=`echo $line |cut -d"," -f3`
    # convert to new date format
    newdate=`echo $date1 | awk '{ print
substr($0,1,4)"-"substr($0,5,2)"-"substr($0,7,2)"
"substr($0,9,2)":"substr($0,11,2)":"substr($0,13,2)}'`
    # append newly formatted row to output file
    echo "${newdate},${fname},${lname}" >> $outputfile
done
```

The contents of the new dataset is here:

```
2014-08-05 23:46:58,Jane,Smith
2017-08-05 23:46:52,Jack,Jones
2016-08-05 23:46:55,Dave,Stone
2013-08-05 23:46:46,John,Smith
2014-08-05 23:46:49,Jean,Davis
2015-08-05 23:46:37,Thad,Smith
2016-08-05 23:46:38,Jack,Pruit
```

Summary

This chapter introduced the `awk` command, which is essentially an entire programming language packaged into a single Unix command.

We explored some of its built-in variables as well as conditional logic, while loops, and `for` loops in `awk` in order to manipulate the rows and columns in datasets. You then saw how to delete lines and merge lines in datasets, and also how to print the contents of a file as a single line of text. Next you learned how to use meta characters and character sets in awk commands. You learned how to perform numeric calculations (such as addition, subtraction, multiplication, and division) in files containing numeric data, and also some numeric functions that are available in awk.

In addition, you saw how to align columns in a dataset, how to delete columns, how to select a subset of columns from a dataset, and how to work with multiline records in datasets. Finally, you saw a couple of simple use cases involving nested quotes and date formats in a structured dataset.

At this point you have all the tools necessary to do quite sophisticated data cleansing and processing, and it is strongly encouraged that you try to apply them on some task or problem of interest. The final step of the learning process is doing something real.

"I saw something similar once, I wonder if there is a way to . . ." or the even more common "how do I do XXX in language YYY?" You can't ask those questions if you don't have a sense of what is possible.

At this point there is one more thing to say: congratulations! You have completed a fast-paced yet dense book, and if you are a bash neophyte, the material will probably keep you busy for many hours. The examples in the chapters provide a solid foundation, and the Appendix contains additional examples and use cases to further illustrate how the Unix commands work together. The combined effect demonstrates that the universe of possibilities is larger than the examples in this book, and ultimately they will spark ideas in you. Good luck!

OTHER CODE SAMPLES

This appendix contains an assortment of bash scripts that illustrate how to solve some well-known tasks, such as recursion-based solutions for the GCD and LCM of two positive integers, as well as awk commands for processing multiple datasets in order to perform arithmetic calculations.

The shell scripts are grouped corresponding to their respective chapters: for instance, awk -related bash scripts are listed as part of the section for Chapter 5. In some cases (such as Chapter 1), N/A is listed when there are no samples for a chapter. Please keep in mind that there is fairly light coverage (in terms of explanations) for the code samples in this Appendix: the assumption is that you have read the code samples in the chapters, thereby enabling you to understand the code without in-depth explanations.

Examples for Chapter 1

N/A

Examples for Chapter 2

The examples in this Appendix for Chapter 2 contains the following shell scripts for calculating Fibonacci numbers, the GCD and LCM of two positive integers, and the divisors of a positive integer:

- Fibonacci.sh
- gcd.sh
- lcm.sh
- Divisors2.sh

Calculating Fibonacci Numbers

Listing A.1 displays the contents of `Fibonacci.sh` that computes the Fibonacci value of a positive integer.

LISTING A.1: Fibonacci.sh

```
#!/bin/sh
LOGFILE="/tmp/a1"
rm -f $LOGFILE 2>/dev/null


fib()
{
     if [ "$1" -gt 3 ]
     then
      echo "1 = $1 2 = $2 3 = $3" >> $LOGFILE

        decr1=`expr $2 - 1`
        decr2=`expr $3 - 1`
        decr3=`expr $3 - 2`
     echo "d1 = $decr1 d2 = $decr2 d3 = $decr3" >> $LOGFILE
        fib1=`fib $2 $3 $decr2`
        fib2=`fib $3 $decr2 $decr3`
        fib=`expr $fib1 + $fib2`
        echo $fib
     else
      if [ "$1" -eq 3 ]
      then
        echo 2
      else
        echo 1
        fi
    fi
}
echo "Enter a number: "
read num
```

```
# add code to ensure it's a positive integer

if [ "$num" -lt 3 ]
then
  echo "fibonacci $num = 1"
else
  decr1=`expr $num - 1`
  decr2=`expr $num - 2`
  echo "fibonacci $num = `fib $num $decr1 $decr2`"
fi
```

In case you don't already know, the Fibonacci sequence is defined as follows:

```
F(1) = 1; F(2) = 2; and F(n) = F(n-1) + F(n-2) for n >= 2.
```

Listing A.1 looks complicated, but in a sense it "extends" the technique shown in Listing 2.10 in Chapter 2. In particular, the code for calculating factorial values involves decrementing one variable, whereas calculating Fibonacci numbers involves decrementing two variables (which are called decr1 and decr2 in Listing A.1) in order to make recursive invocations of the fib() function.

Calculating the GCD of Two Positive Integers

Listing A.2 displays the contents of the shell script gcd.sh that computes the greatest common divisor of two positive integers.

LISTING A.2 gcd.sh

```
#!/bin/sh

function gcd()
{
  if [ $1 -lt $2 ]
  then
    result=`gcd $2 $1`
    echo $result
  else
    remainder=`expr $1 % $2`
```

```
    if [ $remainder == 0 ]
    then
      echo $2
    else
      echo `gcd $2 $remainder`
    fi
  fi
}

a="4"
b="20"
result=`gcd $a $b`
echo "GCD of $a and $b = $result"

a="4"
b="22"
result=`gcd $a $b`
echo "GCD of $b and $a = $result"

a="20"
b="3"
result=`gcd $a $b`
echo "GCD of $b and $a = $result"

a="10"
b="10"
result=`gcd $a $b`
echo "GCD of $b and $a = $result"
```

Listing A.2 is a straightforward implementation of the Euclidean algorithm (check Wikipedia for details) for finding the GCD of two positive integers. The output from Listing A.2 shows the GCD of 4 and 20, as shown here:

```
GCD of 4 and 20 = 4
GCD of 22 and 4 = 2
GCD of 3 and 20 = 1
GCD of 10 and 10 = 10
```

Calculating the LCM of Two Positive Integers

Listing A.3 displays the contents of the shell script lcm.sh that computes the lowest common multiple (LCM) of two positive integers. This script contains the code in the shell script gcd.sh in order to compute the LCM of two positive integers.

LISTING A.3: lcm.sh

```
#!/bin/sh

function gcd()
{
  if [ $1 -lt $2 ]
  then
    result=`gcd $2 $1`
    echo $result
  else
    remainder=`expr $1 % $2`

    if [ $remainder == 0 ]
    then
      echo $2
    else
      result=`gcd $2 $remainder`
      echo $result
    fi
  fi
}
function lcm()
{
  gcd1=`gcd $1 $2`
  lcm1=`expr $1 / $gcd1`
  lcm2=`expr $lcm1 \* $2`
  echo $lcm2
}
a="24"
b="10"
```

```
result=`lcm $a  $b`
echo "The LCM of $a and $b = $result"


a="10"
b="30"
result=`lcm $a  $b`
echo "The LCM of $a and $b = $result"
```

Notice that Listing A.3 contains the `gcd()` function to compute the GCD of two positive integers. This function is necessary because the next portion of Listing A.3 contains the `lcm()` function that invokes the `gcd()` function, followed by some multiplication steps in order to calculate the LCM of two numbers. The output from Listing A.3 displays the LCM of 10 and 24, as shown here:

```
The LCM of 24 and 10 = 120
The LCM of 10 and 30 = 30
```

Calculating Prime Divisors

Listing A.4 displays the contents of the shell script `Divisors2.sh` that calculates the prime factors of a positive integer.

LISTING A.4: Divisors2.sh

```
#!/bin/sh
function divisors()
{
   div="2"
   num="$1"
   primes=""

   while (true)
   do
     remainder=`expr $num % $div`

     if [ $remainder == 0 ]
     then
       #echo "divisor: $div"
       primes="${primes} $div"
```

```
      num=`expr $num / $div`
   else
      div=`expr $div + 1`
   fi


   if [ $num -eq  1 ]
   then
      break
   fi
done


# use 'echo' instead of 'return'
echo $primes
}

num="12"
primes=`divisors $num`
echo "The prime divisors of $num: $primes"


num="768"
primes=`divisors $num`
echo "The prime divisors of $num: $primes"


num="12345"
primes=`divisors $num`
echo "The prime divisors of $num: $primes"


num="23768"
primes=`divisors $num`
echo "The prime divisors of $num: $primes"
```

Listing A.4 contains the divisors() function that consists primarily of a while loop that checks for the divisors of num (which is initialized as the value of $1). The initial value of div is 2, and each time div divides num, the value of div is appended to the primes string, and num is replaced by num/div. If div does not divide num, div is incremented by 1. Note that the while loop in Listing A.4 terminates when num reaches the value of 1.

The output from Listing A.4 displays the prime divisors of 12, 768, 12345, and 23768, as shown here:

```
The prime divisors of 12: 2 2 3
The prime divisors of 768: 2 2 2 2 2 2 2 2 3
The prime divisors of 12345: 3 5 823
The prime divisors of 23768: 2 2 2 2971
```

The prime factors of 12 and 678 are computed in less than 1 second, but the calculation of the prime factors of 12345 and 23768 is significantly slower.

Examples for Chapter 3

The first example in this section illustrates how to determine which zip files contain SVG documents. The second example in this section shows you how to check the entries in a log file (with simulated values). The third code sample shows you how to use the grep command in order to simulate a relational database consisting of three "tables", each of which is represented by a dataset.

Listing A.5 displays the contents of myzip.sh that produces two lists of files: the first list contains the names of the zip files that contain SVG documents, and the second list contains the names of the zip files that do not contain SVG documents.

LISTING A.5: myzip.sh

```
foundlist=""
notfoundlist=""

for f in `ls *zip`
do
    found=`unzip -v $f |grep "svg$"`
    if [ "$found" != "" ]
    then
        #echo "$f contains SVG documents:"
        #echo "$found"
        foundlist="$f ${foundlist}"
    else
```

```
        notfoundlist="$f ${notfoundlist}"
    fi
  done


  echo "Files containing SVG documents:"
  echo $foundlist| tr ' ' '\n'


  echo "Files not containing SVG documents:"
  echo $notfoundlist |tr ' ' '\n'
```

Listing A.5 searches ("looks inside") zip files for the hard-coded string svg. If you want to search for some other string in a set of zip files, then manually replace this string with that other string. Alternatively, you can prompt users for a search string so you don't need to make manual modifications to the shell script.

For your convenience, Listing A.6 displays the contents of searchstrings. sh that illustrates how to enter one or more strings on the command line, in order to search for those strings in the zip files in the current directory.

LISTING A.6: searchstrings.sh

```
  foundlist=""
  notfoundlist=""

  if [ "$#" == 0 ]
  then
      echo "Usage: $0 <string-list>"
      exit
  fi


      zipfiles=`ls *zip 2>/dev/null`

  if [ "$zipfiles" = "" ]
  then
      echo "*** No zip files in `pwd` ***"
      exit
  fi

  for str in "$@"
  do
```

```
echo "Checking zip files for $str:"
for f in `ls *zip`
do
    found=`unzip -v $f |grep "$str"`
    if [ "$found" != "" ]
    then
        foundlist="$f ${foundlist}"
    else
        notfoundlist="$f ${notfoundlist}"
    fi
done
echo "Files containing $str:"
echo $foundlist| tr ' ' '\n'

echo "Files not containing $str:"
echo $notfoundlist |tr ' ' '\n'
foundlist=""
notfoundlist=""
done
```

Listing A.6 first checks that at least one file is specified on the command line, and then initializes the `zipfiles` variable with the list of zip files in the current directory. If `zipfiles` is null, an appropriate message is displayed.

The next section of Listing A.6 contains a `for` loop that processes each argument that was specified at the command line. For each such argument, another for loop will check for the names of the zip files that contain that argument. If there is a match, then the variable $foundlist is updated, otherwise the $notfoundlist variable is updated. When the inner loop has completed, the names of the matching files and the non-matching files are displayed, and then the outer loop is executed with the next command line argument.

Although the preceding explanation might seem complicated, a sample output from launching Listing A.6 will clarify how the code works:

```
./searchstrings.sh svg abc
Checking zip files for svg:
Files containing svg:

Files not containing svg:
shell-programming-manuscript.zip
```

```
shell-progr-manuscript-0930-2013.zip
shell-progr-manuscript-0207-2015.zip
shell-prog-manuscript.zip
Checking zip files for abc:
Files containing abc:

Files not containing abc:
shell-programming-manuscript.zip
shell-progr-manuscript-0930-2013.zip
shell-progr-manuscript-0207-2015.zip
shell-prog-manuscript.zip
```

If you want to perform the search for zip files in subdirectories, modify the loop as shown here:

```
for f in `find . -print |grep "zip$"`
do
    echo "Searching $f…"
    unzip -v $f |grep "svg$"
done
```

If you have the Java SDK on your machine, you can also use the `jar` command instead of the `unzip` command, as shown here:

```
jar tvf $f |grep "svg$"
```

Listing A.7 displays the contents of `skutotals.sh` that calculates the number of units sold for each SKU in `skuvalues.txt`.

LISTING A.7: skutotals.sh

```
SKUVALUES="skuvalues.txt"
SKUSOLD="skusold.txt"

for sku in `cat $SKUVALUES`
do
  total=`cat $SKUSOLD |grep $sku | awk '{total += $2} END
{print total}'`
  echo "UNITS SOLD FOR SKU $sku: $total"
done
```

Listing A.7 contains a `for` loop that iterates through the rows of the file `skuvalues.txt`, and passes those SKU values – one at a time – to a command that involves the `cat`, `grep`, and `awk` commands. The purpose of the latter combination of commands is to 1) find the matching lines in `skusold.txt`, 2) compute the sum of the values of the numbers in the second column, and 3) print the subtotal for the current SKU. In essence, this shell script prints the subtotals for each SKU value.

Launch `skutotals.sh` and you will see the following output:

```
UNITS SOLD FOR SKU 4520: 27
UNITS SOLD FOR SKU 5530: 17
UNITS SOLD FOR SKU 6550: 8
UNITS SOLD FOR SKU 7200: 90
UNITS SOLD FOR SKU 8000: 160
```

We can generalize the previous shell script to take into account different prices for each SKU. Listing A.8 displays the contents of `skuprices.txt`.

LISTING A.8: skuprices.txt

```
4520 3.50
5530 5.00
6550 2.75
7200 6.25
8000 3.50
```

Listing A.9 displays the contents of `skutotals2.sh` that extends the code in Listing A.8 in order to calculate the revenue for each SKU.

LISTING A.9: skutotals2.sh

```
SKUVALUES="skuvalues.txt"
SKUSOLD="skusold.txt"
SKUPRICES="skuprices.txt"

for sku in `cat $SKUVALUES`
do
   skuprice=`grep $sku $SKUPRICES | cut -d" " -f2`
   subtotal=`cat $SKUSOLD |grep $sku | awk '{total += $2} END
{print total}'`
```

```
    total=`echo "$subtotal * $skuprice" |bc`
    echo "AMOUNT SOLD FOR SKU $sku: $total"
done
```

Listing A.9 contains a slight enhancement: instead of computing the subtotals of the number of units for each SKU, the revenue for each SKU is computed, where the revenue for each item equals the price of the SKU multiplied by the number of units sold for the given SKU. Launch skutotals2.sh and you will see the following output:

```
AMOUNT SOLD FOR SKU 4520: 94.50
AMOUNT SOLD FOR SKU 5530: 85.00
AMOUNT SOLD FOR SKU 6550: 22.00
AMOUNT SOLD FOR SKU 7200: 562.50
AMOUNT SOLD FOR SKU 8000: 560.00
```

Listing A.10 displays the contents of skutotals3.sh that calculates the minimum, maximum, average, and total number of units sold for each SKU in skuvalues.txt.

LISTING A.10: skutotals3.sh

```
SKUVALUES="skuvalues.txt"
SKUSOLD="skusold.txt"
TOTALS="totalspersku.txt"
rm -f $TOTALS 2>/dev/null


##############################
#calculate totals for each sku
##############################
for sku in `cat $SKUVALUES`
do
  total=`cat $SKUSOLD |grep $sku | awk '{total += $2} END
{print total}'`
  echo "UNITS SOLD FOR SKU $sku: $total"
  echo "$sku|$total" >> $TOTALS
done

##########################
#calculate max/min/average
##########################
```

```
awk -F"|" '
  BEGIN {first = 1;}
  {if(first) { min = max= avg = sum = $2; first=0; next}}
  { if($2 < min) { min = $2 }
    if($2 > max) { max = $2 }
    sum += $2
  }
  END {print "Minimum = ",min
       print "Maximum = ",max
       print "Average = ",avg
       print "Total   = ",sum
  }
' $TOTALS
```

Listing A.10 initializes some variables, followed by a `for` loop that invokes an `awk` command in order to compute subtotals (i.e., number of units sold) for each `SKU` value. The next portion of Listing A.10 contains an `awk` command that calculates the maximum, minimum, average, and sum for the `SKU` units in the files `$TOTALS`.

Launch the script file in Listing A.10 and you will see the following output:

```
UNITS SOLD FOR SKU 4520: 27
UNITS SOLD FOR SKU 5530: 17
UNITS SOLD FOR SKU 6550: 8
UNITS SOLD FOR SKU 7200: 90
UNITS SOLD FOR SKU 8000: 160
Minimum =  8
Maximum =  160
Average =  27
Total   =  302
```

Simulating Relational Data with the `grep` Command

This section shows you how to combine the `grep` and `cut` commands in order to keep track of a small database of customers, their purchases, and the details of their purchases that are stored in three text files.

Keep in mind that there are many open source toolkits available that can greatly facilitate working with relational data and non-relational data. Those toolkits can be very robust and also minimize the amount of coding that is required.

Moreover, you can use the `join` command (discussed in Chapter 2) to perform SQL-like operations on datasets. Nevertheless, the real purpose of this section is to illustrate some techniques with `grep` that might be useful in your own shell scripts.

Listing A.11 displays the contents of the `MasterOrders.txt` text file.

LISTING A.11: MasterOrders.txt

```
M10000 C1000 12/15/2012
M11000 C2000 12/15/2012
M12000 C3000 12/15/2012
```

Listing A.12 displays the contents of the `Customers.txt` text file.

LISTING A.12: Customers.txt

```
C1000  John  Smith  LosAltos California 94002
C2000  Jane  Davis  MountainView California 94043
C3000  Billy Jones  HalfMoonBay California 94040
```

Listing A.13 displays the contents of the `PurchaseOrders.txt` text file.

LISTING A.13: PurchaseOrders.txt

```
C1000,"Radio",54.99,2,"01/22/2013"
C1000,"DVD",15.99,5,"01/25/2013"
C2000,"Laptop",650.00,1,"01/24/2013"
C3000,"CellPhone",150.00,2,"01/28/2013"
```

Listing A.14 displays the contents of the `MasterOrders.sh` bash script.

LISTING A.14: MasterOrders.sh

```
# initialize variables for the three main files
MasterOrders="MasterOrders.txt"
CustomerDetails="Customers.txt"
PurchaseOrders="PurchaseOrders.txt"

# iterate through the "master table"
for mastCustId in `cat $MasterOrders | cut -d" " -f2`
do
```

```
# get the customer information
custDetails=`grep $mastCustId $CustomerDetails`

# get the id from the previous line
custDetailsId=`echo $custDetails | cut -d" " -f1`


# get the customer PO from the PO file
custPO=`grep $custDetailsId $PurchaseOrders`

# print the details of the customer
echo "Customer $mastCustId:"
echo "Customer Details: $custDetails"
echo "Purchase Orders: $custPO"
echo "----------------------"
echo
done
```

Listing A.14 initializes some variables for orders, details, and purchase-related datasets. The next portion of Listing A.14 contains a for loop that iterates through the id values in the MasterOrders.txt file and uses each id to find the corresponding row in the Customers.txt file as well as the corresponding row in the PurchaseOrders.txt file. Finally, the bottom of the loop displays the details of the information that were retrieved from the initial portion of the for loop. The output from Listing A.14 is here:

```
Customer C1000:
Customer Details: C1000 John Smith LosAltos California 94002
Purchase Orders: C1000,"Radio",54.99,2,"01/22/2013"
C1000,"DVD",15.99,5,"01/25/2013"
----------------------
Customer C2000:
Customer Details: C2000 Jane Davis MountainView California
94043
Purchase Orders: C2000,"Laptop",650.00,1,"01/24/2013"
----------------------
Customer C3000:
Customer Details: C3000 Billy Jones HalfMoonBay California
94040
```

```
Purchase Orders: C3000,"CellPhone",150.00,2,"01/28/2013"
-----------------------
```

Checking Updates in a Logfile

Listing A.15 displays the contents of `CheckLogUpdates.sh` that illustrates how to periodically check the last line in a log file to determine the status of a system. This shell script simulates the status of a system by appending a new row that is based on the current timestamp. The shell script sleeps for a specified number of seconds, and on the third iteration the script appends a row with an error status in order to simulate an error. In the case of a shell script that is monitoring a live system, the error code is obviously generated outside the shell script.

LISTING A.15: CheckLogUpdates.sh

```
DataFile="mylogfile.txt"
OK="okay"
ERROR="error"
sleeptime="2"
loopcount=0
rm -f $DataFile 2>/dev/null; touch $DataFile
newline="`date` SYSTEM IS OKAY"
echo $newline >> $DataFile
while (true)
do
  loopcount=`expr $loopcount + 1`
  echo "sleeping $sleeptime seconds..."
  sleep $sleeptime
  echo "awake again..."
  lastline=`tail -1 $DataFile`
  if [ "$lastline" == "" ]
  then
    continue
  fi
  okstatus=`echo $lastline |grep -i $OK`
  badstatus=`echo $lastline |grep -i $ERROR`
  if [ "$okstatus" != "" ]
  then
```

```
    echo "system is normal"
    if [ $loopcount -lt 5 ]
    then
        newline="`date` SYSTEM IS OKAY"
    else
        newline="`date` SYSTEM ERROR"
    fi
    echo $newline >> $DataFile
elif [ "$badstatus" != "" ]
then
    echo "Error in logfile: $lastline"
    break
fi
done
```

Listing A.15 initializes some variables and then ensures that the log file `mylogfile.txt` is empty. After an initial line is added to this log file, a while loop sleeps periodically and then examines the contents of the final line of text in the log file. New text lines are appended to this log file, and when an error message is detected, the code exits the `while` loop. A sample invocation of Listing A.15 is here:

```
sleeping 2 seconds...
awake again...
system is normal
sleeping 2 seconds...
awake again...
system is normal
sleeping 2 seconds...
awake again...
system is normal
sleeping 2 seconds...
awake again...
system is normal
sleeping 2 seconds...
awake again...
system is normal
sleeping 2 seconds...
awake again...
```

```
Error in logfile: Thu Nov 23 18:22:22 PST 2017 SYSTEM ERROR
```

The contents of the log file are shown here:

```
Thu Nov 23 18:22:12 PST 2017 SYSTEM IS OKAY
Thu Nov 23 18:22:14 PST 2017 SYSTEM IS OKAY
Thu Nov 23 18:22:16 PST 2017 SYSTEM IS OKAY
Thu Nov 23 18:22:18 PST 2017 SYSTEM IS OKAY
Thu Nov 23 18:22:20 PST 2017 SYSTEM IS OKAY
Thu Nov 23 18:22:22 PST 2017 SYSTEM ERROR
```

Examples for Chapter 4

N/A

Examples for Chapter 5

This section of the Appendix contains an assortment of bash scripts that use awk in order to perform various tasks:

1) multiline.sh: convert multi-line records into single-line records
2) sumrows.sh: compute the total of each row in a dataset
3) genetics.sh: an example of the awk 'split' function
4) diagonal.sh: display the main/off-diagonal values and also compute the sum of the main/off-diagonal values
5) calculate column totals from multiple files
6) display main diagonal and off-diagonal values, as well as the sum of those values

The details of these shell scripts are discussed in the following sections.

Processing Multiline Records

Listing A.16 displays the contents of the dataset `multiline.txt` and Listing A.17 displays the contents of the shell script `multiline.sh` that combines multiple lines into a single record.

LISTING A.16: multiline.txt

```
Mary Smith
999 Appian Way
```

```
Roman Town, SF 94234
        Jane Adams
123 Main Street
Chicago, IL 67840
John Jones
321 Pine Road
Anywhere, MN 94949
```

Note that each record spans multiple lines that can contain whitespaces, and records are separated by a blank line.

LISTING A.17: multiline.sh

```
# Records are separated by blank lines
awk '
BEGIN { RS = "" ; FS = "\n" }
{
    gsub(/[ \t]+$/, "", $1)
    gsub(/[ \t]+$/, "", $2)
    gsub(/[ \t]+$/, "", $3)

    gsub(/^[ \t]+/, "", $1)
    gsub(/^[ \t]+/, "", $2)
    gsub(/^[ \t]+/, "", $3)

    print $1 ":" $2 ":" $3 ""
    #printf("%s:%s:%s\n",$1,$2,$3)
}
' multiline.txt
```

Listing A.17 contains a BEGIN block that sets RS ("record separator") as an empty string and FS ("field separator") as a linefeed. Doing so enables us to "slurp" multiple lines into the same record, using a blank line as a separator for different records. The gsub() function removes leading and trailing whitespaces and tabs for three fields in the datasets. The output from launching Listing A.17 is here:

```
Mary Smith:999 Appian Way:Roman Town, SF 94234
Jane Adams:123 Main Street:Chicago, IL 67840
John Jones:321 Pine Road:Anywhere, MN 94949
```

Adding the Contents of Records

Listing A.18 displays the contents of the dataset numbers.txt and Listing A.19 displays the contents of the shell script sumrows.sh that combines and adds the fields in each record.

LISTING A.18: numbers.txt

```
1 2 3 4 5
6 7 8 9 10
5 5 5 5 5
```

LISTING A.19: sumrows.sh

```
awk '{ for(i=1; i<=NF;i++) j+=$i; print j; j=0 }' numbers.txt
```

Listing A.19 contains a simple invocation of the awk command that contains a for loop that uses the variable j to hold the sum of the values of the fields in each record; after which the sum is printed and j is re-initialized to 0. The output from Listing A.19 is here:

```
15
40
25
```

Using the `split` Function in `awk`

Listing A.20 displays the contents of the dataset genetics.txt (some rows wrap across more than one line) and Listing A.21 displays the contents of the shell script genetics.sh that uses the split() function in order to parse the contents of a field in a record.

LISTING A.20: genetics.txt

```
#extract rows with 'gene' and print rows and 'key' value
xyz3    GTF2GFF chro    55555   44444   key=chr1;Name=chr1
xyz3    GTF2GFF gene    77774   11111
key=XYZ123;NB=standard;Name=extra
xyz3    GTF2GFF exon    71874   12227   Super=NR_55555
xyz3    GTF2GFF exon    72613   12721   Super=NR_55555
xyz3    GTF2GFF exon    83221   14408   Super=NR_55555
xyz3    GTF2GFF gene    84362   29370
key=WASH7P;Note=extra;Name=ALPHA
xyz3    GTF2GFF exon    84362   14829   Super=NR_222222
```

LISTING A.21: genetics.sh

```
# required output:
#xyz3:77774:XYZ123
#xyz3:84362:WASH7P
awk -F" " '
{
  if( $3 == "gene" ) {
    split($6, triplet, /[;=]/)
    printf("%s:%s:%s\n", $1, $4, triplet[2] )
  }
}
' genetics.txt
```

Listing A.21 matches input lines whose third field equals gene, after which the array triplet is populated with the components of the sixth field, using the characters ";" and "=" as delimiters in the sixth field. The output consists of the first field, the fourth field, and the second element in the array triplet. The output from launching Listing A.21 is here:

```
xyz3:77774:XYZ123
xyz3:84362:WASH7P
```

Scanning Diagonal Elements in Datasets

Listing A.22 displays the contents of the dataset diagonal.txt and Listing A.23 displays the contents of the shell script diagonal.sh that displays the elements in the main diagonal and off-diagonal, and also computes the sum of the elements in the main diagonal and off-diagonal.

LISTING A.22: diagonal.csv

```
1,1,1,1,1
5,4,3,2,1
8,8,1,8,8
5,4,3,2,1
1,6,6,7,7
```

LISTING A.23: diagonal.sh

```
# NF is the number of fields in the current record.
# NR is the number of the current record/line
```

```
# (not the number of records in the file).
# In the END block (or the last line of the file)
# it's the number of lines in the file.
# Solution in R: https://gist.github.com/dsparks/3693115
echo "Main diagonal:"
awk -F"," '{ for (i=0; i<=NF; i++) if (NR >= 1 && NR == i)
print $(i) }' diagonal.csv
echo "Off diagonal:"
awk -F"," '{print $(NF+1-NR)}' diagonal.csv
echo "Main diagonal sum:"
awk -F"," '
BEGIN { sum = 0 }
{
   for (i=0; i<=NF; i++) { if (NR >= 1 && NR == i) { sum += $i
} }
}
END { printf ("sum = %s\n",sum) }
' diagonal.csv
echo "Off diagonal sum:"
awk -F"," '
BEGIN { sum = 0 }
{
   for (i=0; i<=NF; i++) { if(NR >= 1 && i+NR == NF+1) { sum +=
$i; } }
}
END { printf ("sum = %s\n",sum) }
' diagonal.csv
```

Listing A.23 starts with an `awk` command that contains a loop that matches "diagonal" elements of the dataset, which is to say the first field of the first record, the second field of the second record, the third field of the third record, and so forth. This matching process is handled by the conditional logic inside the `for` loop.

The second part of Listing A.23 contains an `awk` command that prints the off-diagonal elements of the dataset, using a very simple print statement.

The third part of Listing A.23 contains an `awk` command that contains the same logic as the first `awk` command, and then calculates the cumulative sum of the diagonal elements.

The fourth part of Listing A.23 contains an `awk` command that contains logic that is similar to the first `awk` command, with the following variation:

```
if(NR >= 1 && i+NR == NF+1)
```

The preceding logic enables us to calculate the cumulative sum of the off-diagonal elements. The output from launching Listing A.23 is here:

```
Main diagonal:
1
4
1
2
7
Off diagonal:
1
2
1
4
1
Main diagonal sum:
sum = 15
Off diagonal sum:
sum = 9
```

Listing A.24, Listing A.25, and Listing A.26 display the contents of the dataset `rain1.csv`, `rain2.csv`, and `rain3.csv.txt` that are used in several shell scripts in this section.

LISTING A.24: *rain1.csv*

```
1,0.10,53,15
2,0.12,54,16
3,0.19,65,10
4,0.25,86,23
5,0.18,57,17
6,0.23,79,34
7,0.34,66,21
```

LISTING A.25: rain2.csv

```
1,0.00,63,24
2,0.02,64,25
3,0.09,75,19
4,0.15,66,28
5,0.08,67,36
6,0.13,79,23
7,0.24,68,25
```

LISTING A.26: rain3.csv

```
1,1.00,83,34
2,0.02,84,35
3,1.09,75,19
4,0.15,86,38
5,1.08,87,36
6,0.13,79,33
7,0.24,88,45
```

Adding Values From Multiple Datasets (1)

Listing A.27 displays the contents of the shell script `rainfall1.sh` that adds the numbers in the corresponding fields of several CSV files and displays the results.

LISTING A.27: rainfall1.sh

```
# => Calculate COLUMN averages for multiple files

#columns in rain.csv:
#DOW,inches of rain, degrees F, humidity (%)

#files: rain1.csv, rain2.csv, rain3.csv
echo "FILENAMES:"
ls rain?.csv

awk -F',' '
{
  inches+=$2
```

```
    degrees+=$3
    humidity+=$4
}
END {
    printf("FILENAME: %s\n", FILENAME)
    printf("inches:    %.2f\n", inches/7)
    printf("degrees:   %.2f\n", degrees/7)
    printf("humidity:  %.2f\n", humidity/7)
}
' rain?.csv
```

Listing A.27 calculates the sum of the numbers in three columns (i.e., inches of rainfall, degrees Fahrenheit, and humidity as a percentage) in the datasets specified by the expression `rain?.csv`, which in this particular example consists of the datasets `rain1.csv`, `rain2.csv`, and `rain3.csv`. Thus, Listing A.27 can handle multiple datasets (`rain1.csv` through `rain9.csv`). You can generalize this example to handle any dataset that starts with the string `rain` and ends with the suffix `csv` with the following expression:

```
rain*.csv
```

The output from launching Listing A.27 is here:

```
FILENAMES:
rain1.csv   rain2.csv   rain3.csv
inches:     0.83
degrees:    217.71
humidity:   79.43
```

Adding Values From Multiple Datasets (2)

Listing A.28 displays the contents of the shell script `rainfall12.sh` that adds the numbers in the corresponding fields of several CSV files and displays the results.

LISTING A.28: rainfall2.sh

```
# => Calculate ROW averages for multiple files


#columns in rain.csv:
#DOW,inches of rain, degrees F, humidity (%)
```

```
#files: rain1.csv, rain2.csv, rain3.csv

awk -F',' '
{
  mon_rain[FNR]+=$2
  mon_degrees[FNR]+=$3
  mon_humidity[FNR]+=$4
  idx[FNR]++
}
END {
  printf("DAY INCHES DEGREES HUMIDITY\n")

  for(i=1; i<=FNR; i++){
    printf("%3d %-6.2f %-8.2f %-7.2f\n",
      i,mon_rain[i]/idx[i],mon_degrees[i]/idx[i],mon_humidity[i]/
      idx[i])
  }
}
' rain?.csv
```

Listing A.28 is similar to Listing A.27, except that this code sample uses the value of FNR in order to calculate the average rainfall, degrees Fahrenheit, and percentage humidity only for Monday. The output from launching Listing A.28 is here:

```
DAY INCHES DEGREES HUMIDITY
  1 0.37   66.33    24.33
  2 0.05   67.33    25.33
  3 0.46   71.67    16.00
  4 0.18   79.33    29.67
  5 0.45   70.33    29.67
  6 0.16   79.00    30.00
  7 0.27   74.00    30.33
```

Listing A.29, Listing A.30, and Listing A.31 display the contents of the dataset zain1.csv, zain2.csv, and rainz.csv.txt that are used in an upcoming shell script in this section.

LISTING A.29: zain1.csv

```
1,0.10,53,15
2,0.12,54,16
3,0.19,65,10
4,0.25,86,23
5,0.18,57,17
6,0.23,79,34
7,0.34,66,21
```

LISTING A.30: zain2.csv

```
1,0.00,63,24
2,0.02,64,25
3,0.09,75,19
4,0.15,66,28
5,0.08,67,36
6,0.13,79,23
7,0.24,68,25
```

LISTING A.31: zain3.csv

```
1,1.00,83,34
2,0.02,84,35
3,1.09,75,19
4,0.15,86,38
5,1.08,87,36
6,0.13,79,33
7,0.24,88,45
```

Adding Values From Multiple Datasets (3)

Listing A.32 displays the contents of the shell script `rainfall3.sh` that adds the numbers in the corresponding fields of several CSV files and displays the results.

LISTING A.32: rainfall3.sh

```
# => Calculate COLUMN averages for multiple files (backtick)

#columns in rain.csv:
#DOW,inches of rain, degrees F, humidity (%)
```

```
# specify the list of CSV files (supports multiple regexs)
files=`ls rain*csv zain*csv`

echo "FILES: `echo $files`"

awk -F',' '
{
  mon_rain[FNR]+=$2
  mon_degrees[FNR]+=$3
  mon_humidity[FNR]+=$4
  idx[FNR]++
}
END {
  printf("DAY INCHES DEGREES HUMIDITY\n")

  for(i=1; i<=FNR; i++){
    printf("%3d %-6.2f %-8.2f %-7.2f\n",
    i,mon_rain[i]/idx[i],mon_degrees[i]/idx[i],mon_humidity[i]/
    idx[i])

  }

}
' `echo $files`
```

Listing A.32 performs the same calculations as Listing A.28, with the following variation: the datasets specified by the variable `files` that is defined by the regular expression ``ls rain*csv zain*csv``. You can modify this regular expression to include any list of files that need to be processed. Notice that the final line of code in Listing A.32 uses back-tick substitution to expand the regular expression in the definition of the variable `files`:

```
' `echo $files`
```

As yet another variation, you can specify a file – let's call it `filelist. txt` – that contains a list of filenames that you want to process, and then replace the preceding line as follows:

```
' `cat filelist.txt`
```

The output from launching Listing A.32 is here:

```
FILES: rain1.csv rain2.csv rain3.csv zain1.csv zain2.csv
zain3.csv
DAY INCHES DEGREES HUMIDITY
  1 0.37    66.33    24.33
  2 0.05    67.33    25.33
  3 0.46    71.67    16.00
  4 0.18    79.33    29.67
  5 0.45    70.33    29.67
  6 0.16    79.00    30.00
  7 0.27    74.00    30.33
```

Calculating Combinations of Field Values

Listing A.33 displays the contents of the shell script `linear-combo.sh` that computes various linear combinations of the columns in multiple datasets and displays one combined dataset as the output.

LISTING A.33: linear-combo.sh

```
# => combinations of columns
awk -F',' ' '
{
  $2 += $3 * 2 + $4 / 2
  $3 += $4 / 3 + $2 * $2 / 10
  $4 += $2 + $3
  $1 += $2 * 3 - $4 / 10
  printf("%d,%.2f,%.2f,%.2f\n",$1,$2,$3,$4)
}
' rain?.csv
```

Listing A.33 processes the values of the datasets `rain1.csv`, `rain2.csv`, and `rain3.csv` whose contents are shown earlier in this section. The key observation to make is that the sequence of calculations in the calculations in the body of the `awk` statement involved inter-dependencies.

Specifically, the value of `$2` is a linear combination of the values of `$3` and `$4`. Next, the value of `$3` is a linear combination of the value of `$4` and `$2`, where the latter is *not* the original value from the datasets, but its calculated value. Third, the value of $4 is a linear combination of $2 and of $3, both of which are calculated values and not the values in the datasets. Finally, the value of $1 is a linear combination of the newly calculated values for $2 and $4.

As you can see, awk provides the flexibility to specify practically any combination of calculations (including non-linear combinations) in a very simple and sequential fashion. The output of Listing A.33 is here:

```
194,113.60,1348.50,1477.10
196,116.12,1407.72,1539.84
204,135.19,1895.97,2041.16
187,183.75,3470.07,3676.82
202,122.68,1567.70,1707.38
194,175.23,3160.89,3370.12
207,142.84,2113.33,2277.17
201,138.00,1975.40,2137.40
202,140.52,2046.92,2212.44
201,159.59,2628.23,2806.82
203,146.15,2211.32,2385.47
203,152.08,2391.83,2579.91
199,169.63,2964.10,3156.73
206,148.74,2288.69,2462.43
183,184.00,3479.93,3697.93
182,185.52,3537.43,3757.95
200,160.59,2660.25,2839.84
179,191.15,3752.50,3981.65
178,193.08,3826.99,4056.07
195,174.63,3139.56,3347.19
173,198.74,4052.76,4296.50
```

Summary

In this appendix, you saw examples of how to use some useful and versatile bash commands. First you saw examples of shell scripts for various tasks involving recursion, such as computing the GCD (greatest common divisor) and the LCM (lowest common multiple) of two positive integers, the Fibonacci value of a positive integer, and also the prime divisors of a positive integer.

Next you saw a bash script with the grep command, a while loop, and other constructs that append data to a log file, with logic to determine when to exit the bash script. In addition, you learned how to use the grep command to simulate a simple relational database.

In the final portion of this Appendix you learned how to use awk to process records that span multiple lines, how to compute column sums and averages involving multiple datasets, and how to use awk -related functions such as gsub() and split(). Finally, you learned how to dynamically calculate various combinations of columns of numbers from multiple datasets.

INDEX